D0482668

WORDS

AND THEIR WAYS

An Introduction

to

the Great Words of Western Thought

by

EUGENE H. SLOANE, Ph.D.

Second Edition

THE OWL PRESS

Bay Ridge   1961

Annapolis, Maryland

Copyright, 1955, 1961 by
Eugene H. Sloane

All rights reserved. This book or any part thereof
may not be reproduced in any form without permis-
sion of the author or publisher.

Second Edition

L. C. Cat. Card No.: 61-8625

Printed in the United States of America

PREFACE

This second edition of *Words and Their Ways* requires a new preface. A statement of the contents and purpose of the book has been transferred to "A Word to the Reader." This preface is limited to a brief reply to a few criticisms of the first edition and to a summary of the changes in the present edition.

In "A Word to the Reader" in the first edition the author gave without comment the usual etymology of "etymology" ('ÉTUMOS, real, true, and LÓGOS, word) and thereby unwittingly laid himself open to the charge that he was a victim of "the etymological fallacy;" that is, the assumption that the earlier, and especially the earliest, meanings of a word constitute the "true" meanings. Even a skimming of the book should have revealed the absurdity of the charge.

Two more reasonable criticisms were 1) that the book does not include a number of interesting etymologies, or 2) that it is limited mainly to words of either Greek or Latin derivation.

This book does not include a word just because it has a curious etymology, nor does it attempt to reflect the extent of English borrowings from many different sources.

The writer has deliberately limited himself to those great words which have entered into the main stream of Western thought and on which, aided by certain visual symbols like the circle, the sphere, and the cross, we largely depend to create our inner world of dream and idea and our outer world of the things that are or might be.

Hence it is scarcely surprising that a great number of the words that constitute the English *Logos* have their roots deep in Greek or Latin.

The major changes in this second edition are these:

1. A new subtitle that more accurately conveys an idea of the contents.

2. A new preface and a new "Word to the Reader."

3. Additions to the two final chapters to deal a little more adequately with certain aspects of religion, which, in the first edition, because of publishing exigencies, were treated with unbecoming brevity.

4. A full word index to make the book more helpful to students and teachers.

It should be mentioned, in addition, that a good many errors were corrected in the successive printings of the first edition and in this edition. No doubt still others continue to enjoy their obscurantist existence in the shadows cast by black on white; and the writer is always pleased, if, at times, a little red-faced, to have them called to his attention.

Grateful thanks are due to Professor Frank C. Becker for his help and encouragement and to many former students from whom the writer learned.

Eugene H. Sloane

Bay Ridge
December, 1960

TABLE OF CONTENTS

Chapter	Page
A Word to the Reader	1
1. Nearer Than Hands and Feet	3
2. Hear Ye!	9
3. Vision	14
4. Sign and Symbol	20
5. Kith and Kin	23
6. Substance	29
7. Reality	35
8. Return to Earth	42
9. Twists of the Tongue	45
10. By Way of Analogy	52
11. Reason and Vision	57
12. Doing Things	63
13. All Good Acts	70
14. Beautiful Things	78
15. The Many and the Few	82
16. First and Last Things	89
17. God's Voices	93
18. One	105

To

Aphrodite, Winifred, and White Wave
for they are one and the same

A WORD TO THE READER

WORDS AND THEIR WAYS is intended for anyone interested in learning how to use words with full awareness of both their powers and limitations.

It invites you to take a second and more careful look at the little words you assume you know—little words like "matter," "nature," "pretty," "substance," and "love." It also introduces you to most of the important words of literature, science, philosophy, and religion and shows how they are compounded of the same little ordinary words that we use every day.

Each chapter deals with the words pertaining to a basic category of thought. For example, Chapter 5, "Kith and Kin," deals with those words that pertain to scientific classification and philosophical generalization, and Chapter 13, "All Good Acts," deals with the terms and problems of ethical behavior.

By uncovering a word's etymological roots and by relating it to other more familiar terms in the same category of meaning, the book gives you a grasp of the meanings that matter—those that determine the way we view the world, those that, in large measure, really create the kind of a mind we have. The attempt has been made to single out only those words—a few less than thirteen hundred[1]—that have affected the thinking of all educated men down through the centuries. Thoroughly master the words you are introduced to in this book, and you will have gone a long way on the road to self-education, the best kind of all.

[1] By actual count of the Word Index, 812 English words, 284 Latin words, and 194 Greek words—1290 in all.

The book may be read in several ways. You can select a single chapter at random and read it in odd moments. If you have developed a distaste for philosophy, you might find the going easier by beginning with Chapter 9, reading on to the end, and then reading Chapters 1-8. But, of course, the best way is to read carefully right straight through to get the plot. For this is a book with a plot; and if you are a reasonably good reader, you will uncover it.

Properly read, you should put this book down with a feeling of intellectual emancipation. The great words of Western thought will have flowed through your mind and broken down old, and, largely unconscious, habitual bonds of opinion and illusion; and you will have experienced a re-vitalization of your mind. You will also have discovered that, as the writer has said elsewhere, " . . . words are candles to see with, not idols to bow before, and ought to be moved about and trimmed frequently."[2]

A simplified system of spelling Greek words with the English alphabet makes the book easy reading for those who know no Greek. All Greek words are in English small capitals, and all Latin words are in italic letters. In the Word Index, Greek words appear in both English small capitals and the Greek alphabet for the convenience of those who would like to consult a Greek lexicon.

One more word of advice. Often, without warning or labeling, words will be used playfully, including good and bad puns. This twisting of words is done partly to illustrate the variety of meanings that have accrued to a word, partly to free you from thralldom to habitual association and acceptance of one bond of meaning. Often very weighty matters will be handled with levity.

[2] *Psychology for Living* (Annapolis: 1957), p. 124.

2

CHAPTER 1

NEARER THAN HANDS AND FEET

There have been three great concerns of mankind and, hence, three great philosophical questions: What is *real?* What is *true?* What is *good?* The branch of philosophy that attempts to answer each of these questions is called, respectively, *ontology, epistemology,* and *ethics.* We shall look more closely at the meaning of each of these words later on.

For many reasons the big question in philosophy for the past three hundred years has been the second of these questions, the epistemological one: What is true? No one would ever raise that question until he had begun to doubt his ability to know real things. The question rephrased amounts to: How can I be sure that I can know "The Truth"? And this amounts to: How can I be sure that I can distinguish real and good things from unreal and bad things?

A child, a well-adjusted successful and happy man, or a madman would never be bothered by such a question. It takes a somewhat maladjusted man rather sharply aware of the difference between himself and the other things around him, aware of their opposition and hostility, and aware that the times are out of joint.

As we are living in such a world and most of us have a fairly acute awareness of the fact, we shall begin our study of words and their ways by taking the customary

---

* In this and the remaining chapters Latin words will be in Italics, Greek words in small capitals.

path through the epistemological woods. Though the path that we shall follow is an old one, our vehicle will be out of the ordinary.

In making a beginning of this kind it is also customary to subject to examination those sensitive instruments that register *some* of the things going on in and around us—traditionally the five, but really the ten or more, senses. However, let us begin with something more physical, more intimate, and, in a way, even more sensual than the senses, something nearer than hands and feet—our muscles. Can we by the stretching of our muscles build a chain of being and reach heaven? We can and we will.

In so many ways it is good to begin with our muscles, though the etymology is not so illuminating, except to teach us that many things get their names quite by accident. "Muscle" comes from *musculus,* "little mouse," because of a fancied resemblance between them; and *musculus* comes from a Sanscrit root *Mush,* "to steal," because, of course, the mouse is "the stealing one."

It is with and by our muscles that we move and live and have our being. Some may laugh with H. L. Mencken at what he called "the striated muscle cult" in America, and certainly its commercialized excesses must be deplored, but all of our endeavors depend ultimately on our muscles, whether striated or smooth or that unique mixed muscle called the heart.

In their functioning, muscles contract and relax, and locomotion is possible because one set contracts while another set relaxes, thus exhibiting so beautifully the principle of contradiction that is at the heart of all motion in the universe and offering us a clue to both the nature and the tragicomedy of existence.

4

"Contract" comes from the Latin *contraho,* "to draw together," and "relax" from *relaxo,* "to stretch out again" or "to unloosen again." Another name for contraction is "tension," of which there is so much in our modern world. "Tension" is derived from *tendo* and the Greek τείνο, both of which mean "to stretch," "to draw tight," "to strain." "Strain" comes from *stringo* and στράγγω, which also mean "to draw tight."

A cord or wire is tense when drawn "taut," which comes from a Teutonic word that also means "to draw" or "to pull." A hunting bow is "tense" or "taut" because its ends are drawn into a position contrary to the forces determining its rigidity and straightness.

Muscles become tense through a similar tug of contrary forces. Healthy muscles should possess "tensility," that is, the capability of being "tense." However, if the condition is too great and prolonged, it is called "tonic spasm," which is a symptom of diseases like *tetanus* and *polio,* or "rigor mortis," which is a symptom of a disease called *death.*

"Spasm" comes from σπάο, which means "to draw tight;" and "tonic," as you must have already guessed, comes from the same verbs as "tension," namely, *tendo* and τείνο. A "tense" violin string has "tonicity"—has "tone." And a properly "toned" muscle has "tonicity." If you drink a "tonic," it may help "tone" up your system and give your muscles "tonicity" and "tensility"! Healthy muscles should have these two characteristics, but they should not become "spastic" (from σπάο, to draw tight) or "convulsed," which comes from *convello,* "to pluck" or "to pull violently."

"Convulse" is to "contract" what "spasm" is to "tension." The ways of language are often wayward. We

5

say "convulsed with laughter" and not "contracted with laughter," though the former has the more morbid overtone of "spasm."

All of these various terms for "draw tight" that have passed into popular and medical usage serve to distinguish two kinds of "drawing tight," one normal and healthy and the other abnormal and harmful. The difference between them is, to put it as simply as possible, the difference between enough and too much, which is another way of stating the Golden Mean of the Ancient Greeks, "Nothing in excess."

Our muscles give us not only locomotion and mute admonitions regarding the need for harmony and balance but also our most intimate feelings about such great words as "force," "energy," "gravity," and "work" —indeed, so much so that whatever scientists may say about "force" or "energy" in abstract mathematical equations, we know the *feel* of force and energy in the act of exerting (*exsero,* to stretch out, to thrust out) ourselves in opposition to an opponent force, whether another muscle or something extraneous, and becoming tense.

Muscles produce force in both its original and derived senses. "Force" is from *fortis,* the Sanscrit root of which means "to be courageous," and *fortis* means "courageous," "brave," and "stout-hearted." So it is quite logical, if not always inevitable, that a muscular man is a brave man, a stout-hearted fellow, possessed of fortitude, that is, strength to withstand adversity or adverse force.

Muscles at work are measured by scientists in ergs, from 'ÉRGON, "work," "a man's business," "employment." and such measurement involves the employment (derived from *implico,* involve!) of one instrument to measure another, for a muscle is an organ, and an 'ÓRGANON is an instrument, a tool for work. Aristotle's works on logic called *The Organon,* the organs of the body, the house organ of a company, and the musical instrument called an organ are all instrumentalities for certain kinds of work.

When muscles are at rest, they are, speaking etymologically, like dynamite (DÝNAMIS, strength, potentially vigorous), and when they are in dynamic action as we use the word "dynamic," they are actually energetic ('ENERGÉO, to work, to be active). "Act," "action," "actually," and "active," it must be added, derive from *actio,* a doing or performing, and an *actor* is one who puts a thing in motion. Muscles at rest have the potentiality of being potent (*potens,* able, mighty, powerful), and muscles at work are actually actors and actually active.

It is by our muscles that we first put things and men to the test by trying them out. One way to try them out is to experiment, which comes from *experior,* to try thoroughly, to test. *Perior,* PERÁO, and PRÁSSO all mean "to go or pass through," and the third also means "to achieve or bring about" and "to practice a business or a trade." PRÂGMA, the noun, means "that which has been done," "the deed," and hence, "matter," "fact," or "business."

If we try enough things thoroughly, that is, experiment, we shall, of course, gain experience. An experience is an experiment, and many experiments are also called experience. The muscles that pass through and complete journeys and experiment are the first and semi-eternal pragmatists. They believe in practice or praxis and scorn theory (THEÁOMAI, to view, gaze at, behold), which is only to be expected because they cannot see.

The sense of the muscles is feeling, or, more accurately, kinesthesia. This compound word speaks for itself when it is taken apart. KINÉO means "to set into motion," "to move," which is what the cinema does, and 'ÁISTHESIS is the Greek equivalent of *sensus,* from which we get the word that means them, "sensation." Kinesthesia, then, is the sensation of movement.

"Feeling," a more general term comprehending the senses of pain, temperature, and kinesthesia, comes from the same root that gave rise to PALÁME, and "palm," meaning in all three tongues both a part of the hand and the hand itself. Feeling is a palming or handling activity, a trying or testing by touching.

The derivation of "touch" is obscure—as is true of so many of the "palpable" words—but it is connected, so it would seem, with the act of knocking.

Let us accept this as a sign of promise, for how true it is that in the beginning, like a blindfolded neophyte (NÉOS, new, and PHYTÓS, grown) knocking at the outer door of the Grand Lodge, we knock upon the world, asking for admission so that we may hear a friendly voice and behold the light.

Chapter 2

HEAR YE!

The first voice (*vox,* from *voco,* to call out) that we hear coming from the other side of the door on which we knock *is* a friendly one.

Having labored and delivered and feeling once more the sap of life flowing upward, the mother looks down at the helpless creature beside her and, in response to its feeble knocking on her flesh, gives it meat and drink and voices loving sounds.

At this moment a community is born.

Goodness knows the origin of language. There are a dozen or more theories that have their spokesmen today, but we are partial to one. Speech—language— began through the efforts of the mothers to share their experiments in living with their children. Men have written history and they have given it a bias in their favor, but we incline to Briffault's position: the mothers formed the community.

Even the barnyard will teach us this, if we will stop and watch and listen. The rooster is busy crowing about some odd conceit of his; the hen says "cluck! cluck!" and her chicks come arunning. A friendly voice is communicating and forming for a moment, at least, a little community, a commune, or a commonwealth as she and they share one with the other. For these words communicate the meaning of *communico* and *communis,* from which they, as well as the adjective "common," are derived.

9

In time, a long tale of time, these friendly communal cries gave rise to the languages of mankind. *Lingo* is the Latin for "lick" and that which licks is the *lingua,* the tongue. The tongues of men create the tongues whereby men communicate, that is, share, their individual experiments in living.

A Greek verb for say and speak is MYTHÉOMAI. MŶTHOS, from whence our "myth," is anything spoken— a speech, a command, a tale, and, later, a legendary tale. The Latin equivalent of MŶTHOS is *fabula,* which is derived from the verb *for,* to say or speak. And English "tale" comes from an Old Teutonic verb that means to say, speak, tell, or reckon.

Tales, fables, myths were the first fruits of speech. They could be based on fact, hearsay, dream, or vision. A later development was history, which in its Greek original, ʽISTORÍA, is information learned by inquiry and an account of such learning by inquiry. Our "story," though it derives from the same source, has a meaning closer to "tale," "fable," and "myth."

"In the beginning was the Word and the Word was with God and the Word was God"—this is probably the most quoted and least understood verse in the whole New Testament. What does it mean?

In the Latin it is: *In Principio erat Verbum, et Verbum erat apud Deum, et Deus erat Verbum.* In Greek, the language in which the Gospel of John was first written, it goes:

Ἐν ἀρχῇ ἦν ὁ λόγος καὶ ὁ λόγος
ἦν πρὸς τὸν θεόν καὶ θεὸς ἦν ὁ λόγος.

We shall not dare attempt an interpretation. For our purpose we are interested in only one word anyway; this is *Verbum* or LÓGOS. What does it mean? A teacher in a class in a certain college, attempting to offer a synonym for it, so shook the faith of a young divinity student that he withdrew from that college. "Logos" is a big word—so big that by the time the author of John appropriated it, it was already loaded with philosophical and theological meanings, as the reader can discover for himself by consulting the article, *Logos,* in the *Encyclopaedia Britannica.*

Here let us remain content with what the Greek dictionary has to say about λόγος. Back of it is λέγο, and λέγο means to lay, to lay asleep, to lay in order, to reckon and count, to say, speak, utter. Laying sounds in order is to speak. And speech, that which is said or spoken, is λόγος. "Logomachy" (λόγος plus μάχε, battle, fight) is a quarrel over words; monologue and dialogue speak for themselves.

Consequently, the translation of λόγος as "Word" is not very satisfactory for many reasons, one being that the Greeks did not think of speech as being composed of separate words as we do. Speech also means inner speech or "reason," and λόγος also means this, but we shall have to dialecticize (δια-λέγο) about this weighty matter later on.

Primitive and ancient man had more faith in the power of speech than we have today. To know the name of a thing was to *know* it—and also to have power over it. "Name" itself bears witness to this belief. It comes from *nomen,* which in its primitive sense means the thing serving for knowing an object by. And *nomen* itself comes from *nosco* or *gnosco,* to know.

"What's in a name?" Ancient peoples would reply, "Everything." Even their folk-lore and religion grew out of place-names. Gods had names that were never

11

spoken. "Jehovah" was a mistaken attempt of translators to make a pronounceable name out of what in the original Hebrew was a four-letter sign standing for the unutterable name of the Lord of Hosts. And primitive peoples the world over won't name their true names lest an enemy gain power over them.

A name, a sound of the voice, can be "univocal," that is, stand for one thing only. But it can be "equivocal," the same sound standing for two or more different things. A "page" can be a leaf of a book or a youth preparing for knighthood. A "key" can be a reef, a lock-opener, a tone of voice, a summary of difficult material, or a part of a piano. This possibility for equivocation provides material for puns, but it is also one of the causes of confusion among men.

It is not easy to share experience under the best of conditions. The difficulties are much greater when men must depend on tongues and ears to transmit the experiments in living. Then those living in another valley over the mountain may speak a strange, outlandish tongue and deserve the name "barbarian" (BÁRBAROS, one who babbles or stammers) ; and, being outside the pale of the community, those inside are privileged to stone or, enslave them.

Prints in the sand are evanescent signs of something, but they are not so evanescent as the fleeting sounds of speech. The vocalized sound "points" to something as a finger can point, but there is only rarely anything in common between the sound and the thing it points to. What in common have the sound "world" and the object that it singles out for someone to mind?

"What do you mean?" cries the ear; and the tongue

replies, "I mean . . .," and the misunderstanding increases.

To "mean" comes from the Indo-European root *Men-, Mon-, Mn-* that became Greek MNÉME (remembrance, memory, recollection) , Latin *mens,* and English "mind." So I *mean* what I *mind,* but does the auditor ('AÛS, ear) mind what you mean? How can we know for sure when the sign is a sound that is intended to design (mark out) or designate an object or, worse still, another sound that is not uttered aloud but only whispered internally, which we call a "thought?"

"What does your sound signify?" the ear says.

"Something very significant," the tongue replies.

"I don't get it," says the ear. "Try another signal."

The tongue is momentarily tongue-tied.

"If you will show me a sign it will greatly help," the auditor says.

"I was coming to that," the speaker says. "But please open your eyes so that you can see the semaphore (SÊMA, sign, plus FÉRO, to bear, carry) that I make with my hands."

The speaker points to an object and says, "I mean this."

"*Now* I see the significance of your remarks. They are now semantic (SEMANTIKÓS, significant, from SEMAÍNO, to show or point out) .

CHAPTER 3

VISION

Feeling and hearing must take second place to vision as the gateway to union with the real; and many words in Greek, Latin, and English bear witness to the identification of seeing with truth. "Seeing is believing," says the old saw. A wise man is a man of vision. Even the sentence is a tautology, as is true of so much that we say. "Wise" and "wit" (to wit, I wist not) come from the Indo-European root that means "to see." Etymologically, the sentence says, "A seeing man is a man of vision." How true!

Since vision is *the* way of knowing, and light is the source from whence it comes, all wise men have been, in some important respect, sun and light worshippers. Having sought enlightment, they have tended to look for illumination (*lumen,* light, from *luceo,* to shine) of the darkness about them and for elucidation of their experiments in living from a being residing in the pellucid depths of the sky.

Unfortunately, the test of lucidity is not always enough. Things seen are appearances and phenomena (PHAÍNO, to bring to light, to make clear); and phenomena can even be fantastic (PHANTÁZO, to make clear, visible, manifest). There have been seers of visions who thought they beheld phantasms of the dead. Others, having had similar experiences and having speculated (*specula,* a look-out, a watch-tower, from *specio,* to look at) about such specters, have concluded them to be mere

14

spectacles contrived by dishonest speculators manipulating mirrors.

When one speculates, what does he behold? Obviously, "species," that is, outward appearances, or the shape of things, made by the play of light and shadow on objects. This, of course, is the original Latin meaning, as its source *specio* reveals; and it may seem that there is little in common·between this meaning and the meaning involved in a famous modern book called *The Origin of Species.* This is a misapprehension, as we shall see in a moment.

The early Old English meanings of the noun "shape" are "creation," "creature," "make," and "form;" and of the verb, "shape," "to create," "to fashion," and "to form." "Scop" is early English for poet, who is a "maker" or "shaper." "God is our maker" and "God has shaped us to His ends" are still current phrases. The thing shaped has a shape, by which the eye makes it out.

Morphé is an important Greek word for "shape," "form," and "figure." The verb is morphó, "to form," "to give shape to." Morphology is the science of form. In the field of biology morphology is that branch that deals with the forms of animals and plants, and the structures, homologies, and metamorphoses which govern or influence that form. In the field of philology it is that branch of grammar which is concerned with inflection and word-formation.

The Latin verb *fingo* has most of the meanings of our verb "shape," and the thing shaped is the *figura* or "figure." *Forma,* meaning "contour," "figure," "shape," gave us, of course, "form." "Inform" means "to give form to." God "informs" nature; and, with a shift of meaning, a teacher "informs" the minds of his pupils with "information."

Schêma, which, with very little phonetic change, became our "scheme," was a Greek word for "form," "shape," and "outward appearance." The Ancient Greeks would speak of a "scheme of dress," that is, a "form" or "fashion" of dress. Our "scheme" still echoes these meanings, though not very clearly because of other associations. A "scheme" is a plan or outline for a proposed course of action, usually nefarious, but sometimes, as in "That's a pretty scheme!" fantastic. In a phrase like "the scheme of a poem" and in the verb "schematize," meaning "systematize," the original meaning is more apparent.

Close synonyms for "form" as a verb are "mark," "stamp," "trace," "carve," "engrave," "etch," "mould," "pattern," and so forth, which we need not trace to earlier meanings. The acts signified by these words produce, either as physical objects or mental images, "impressions," "prints," "carvings," "engravings," "stamps," "etchings," "casts," and so on.

The artist etches an etching on copper, and painful events are etched on our hearts. In a somewhat similar fashion light illuminates the objects of the world and the acts of men; and these shapes, cast on the impressionable stuff called the "nervous system" and the "brain," in combination with other impressions like touch and sound, shape an inner world of impressions and forms that we call the "mind." Impressions paid attention to are "minded," and impressions "re-minded" are "re-collections."

The most famous of all words in this class, because of the role it played in Plato's philosophy and in that of

16

his Neo-Platonic descendents, is ʼΕῖΔΟΣ. In philosophy, philology, and theology it is second only to ΛΌΓΟΣ, and yet by one of the greatest ironies of language, the word never got into English in any significant form. From a couple of its close relatives, ʼΕΊΔΟΛΟΝ and ΕΙΚΌΝ, we got "idol," which early Christians linked once and for all with pagan worship of images, and "icon," a much more respectable name for religious images. It is the old story: heathens worship idols; *we* worship in the presence of icons! Oddly or not, worshipers in the presence of icons gave rise to iconoclasts, "idol-breakers!"

ʼΕῖΔΟΣ comes from the verb ʼΕῖΔΟ, which has two different meanings and two different forms, "to see" (ʼΕῖΔΟΝ) and "to know" (ʼΟῖΔΑ). The Platonic ʼΕῖΔΟΣ is usually translated "idea" or "form" or "archetype," all of which are unsatisfactory. "Idea," which comes from the infinitive form of ʼΕῖΔΟΝ, has a more derogatory meaning than ʼΕῖΔΟΣ, namely, the "look" or "appearance" of a thing as opposed to its "knowability" and "reality." From a Latin form *idealis* comes "ideal," which is a little better, for it communicates some of the "ideas" inherent in Platonism.

The best translation of ʼΕῖΔΟΣ is "notion," for like it "notion" is linked with vision and knowing, "notion" coming from *notio,* an "idea" or "conception," and derives from the same root as *nosco,* to know. Some philosophers, Platonists or otherwise, have in the past used "notion" in this nobler sense; but the genius of the English language is against them: "notions" are held by women and other notionate creatures or even sold at the notion counter.

17

The problem of translating 'ΕΙ̂ΔΟΣ may seem to be a prime example of logomachy, a quarrel over words; but if it is, then so is nearly all philosophy, for the quarrel over the Platonic "forms," "shapes," "examples," or "species" has been a central one in philosophy and has been responsible for the observation that everyone is either a Platonist or Aristotelian. If you are a "Platonist," you hold that there are eternal shapes or patterns, of which all things that the eyeball beholds are feeble copies; if you are an "Aristotelian," you hold that the only shapes there are are those that are the shape of something. An eternal shape that is not the shape of anything is a Cheshire grin, a grin without even a Cheshire cat.

The problem of translating 'ΕΙ̂ΔΟΣ is also a first-class illustration of the difficulties inherent in all attempts to translate one tongue into another. Translation of a poem is simply impossible because the poem, if it be good enough to translate, is good because it grew out of the unique qualities of the language in which it was written. If the translator makes an equally good poem in another language, he has necessarily performed an act of creation rather than of translation. Prose is easier to translate, but if it be philosophic prose, not much easier, for philosophy, like poetry, grows out of the language in which it is written.

One very important word pertaining to shapes and forms and figures we have still to consider: this is "image." While it is so close to "idea" that "mental image" and "idea" are almost synonymous, "image" comes from a considerably different source not so directly connected with the act of seeing. Its immediate source, *imago,* and its root, IM (compare ΜΙΜΕΟΜΑΙ, mimic)

18

embody not only the concept of image or copy of something but also of imitation. An "image" is a mimicking of something, not by sound or gesture, but by a statue, cast, engraving, or picture. A "mental image" is, by analogy, an imitation of reality due to an impression made by a physical object, a sound, or light upon the "wax" of the nervous system and the brain.

"Imagination" is the act of "imaging." The earlier meanings of "image" and "imaging" connect them with *pictura,* a painting, and *pingo,* to represent pictorially with the pencil or needle, to paint or embroider.

Though "images" and "ideas" are impressions of the external world upon us, it should never be forgotten that there is little correspondence between the objects themselves and what they have done to us by putting their stamp upon us anymore than there is a direct correspondence between the fire in a furnace and the thermostat in the room that responds to it.

Ideas and images are really the signatures or marks of nature written upon each of us. We must never, never identify the writer with his signatures. But neither must we make the mistake of the skeptic and conclude that there is no dependable relation between the writing and the writer, nor that of the philosophical idealist and conclude that the writing tells us nothing about the writer but only something about the material on which the writing was done, namely, our own subjective selves.

CHAPTER 4

SIGN AND SYMBOL

When Robinson Crusoe, walking along the shore, discovered footprints in the sand, he read it as an ambiguous sign. Did it signify friend or foe? Signs like sounds can be full of ambiguous significance, even though signs are, for the most part, more permanent than spoken names.

"Sign" comes from *signum,* a mark, token, or sign, the verb *signo* meaning to set a mark upon, to mark, to point out. A red lantern is a sign or signal of danger.

The illiterate man unable to make a proper sign, his signature, on a legal document, is permitted to make his mark. Either mark or signature signifies the author thereof. Documents of state require not only signatures but seals, which comes from *sigillum,* a diminutive form of *signum,* meaning "little figure," that is, the figure on a seal-ring. In former days the impressions of seal- or signet-rings were the signatures, that is, the authentic marks, of great illiterates.

Sêma is the Greek for *signum* or "sign" and from it we got "semaphore" and "semantics." Only certain technicians like railway signalmen and members of the Signal Corps are thought of as users of semaphore. Actually all of us all of the time are busy wig-wagging with vocal and printed signs, trying to share in the human community, trying to get others to understand our signals.

Contemporary writers on semantics like to distinguish **"sig**n" from "symbol" by using the former to designate a symbol that is closer to what it designates, whereas a symbol has little or no similarity to what it signifies. The "sign" in this sense is called a "natural sign." Smoke is a sign of fire and a footprint is a sign of a man; on the other hand, the spoken sound or written character "smoke" is a symbol for smoke and "man" is a symbol for either a single man or men in general.

The distinction is, of course, worth making, but as far as origins go, the terms could be reversed. The origin of "sign" has just been designated. SÝMBOLON, from the verb SYMBÁLLO, to throw together, was a coin or other token which two contracting parties broke and each took half just as today an untrusting person may give half of a bill to someone at the outset of a task and the other half when the task is completed. In ancient Athens a SÝMBOLON was a ticket given to those who attended court, and later upon presenting it, they received payment for their "jury" duty.

"Print," "trace," "sign," "symbol," "mould," "pattern," "figure," "image," *etc.*, all refer to impressions made on something by something, some meaning primarily the former and some the latter. If the latter, they are "signs" or "designs" impressed on some material like paper, cloth, or metal. A flag is a sign of power and authority. A similar kind of sign is "emblem," which is from 'ÉMBLEMA, a thing put on, the verb being 'EMBALLO, to throw in or on. "Type," (TÝPOS), either a blow or marks of a blow, and "emblem" have most of the meanings of "stamp" "cut," and "carve."

When the signs of the tongue, sounds and names, could be stamped, marked, carved, or typed on stones, sticks, skins, or paper, mankind took a tremendous step forward. When the Athenian judges gave those attend-

21

ing court a "symbol," they were visibly, concretely dividing the Athenians into two classes, those attending court and those not attending. A symbol in this original sense is a "ticket" or "label." Theaters still give tickets and laundrymen give labels.

The Chinese laundryman puts some kind of sign or symbol on the collars, shirts, pajamas, handkerchiefs, vests, *etc.*, and it enables him to know that this is the class "Jones." Another symbol on another collection of apparel enables him to know that this is the class "Smith." Thus the laundryman has "generalized" one heterogeneous group of objects from another heterogeneous group of objects. All of these things fall under the "sign," "symbol," "type," "form," "genus," "species," "idea," or 'εἶδος "Jones." All of *these* things fall under the "sign," "symbol," *etc.*, "Smith."

It has been customary to picture mankind's progress in civilization and culture as the "spiritualization" of man, and in a sense this is true; but it is also true that all his forward steps came about as a result of his discovering ways and means to "materialize" his experience and his existence. Carvings, emblems, marks, pictures, and alphabets enabled him to nail down fleeting speech and impressions. Every forward step has depended upon the invention of some physical tool; and, perhaps, the greatest of these was the use of concrete signs in order to organize and generalize experience. Arresting fleeting impressions by impressing them on sticks and stones made possible both a community and the mind of its individual members.

CHAPTER 5

KITH AND KIN

When Darwin chose the word "species" for the title of his epoch-making work, he was no doubt conforming to current nomenclature, but a better word would have been "kinds." "Species," as we have seen, means visible form or structure and, therefore, classes or groupings in accordance with appearances. What Darwin was after was an explanation of classes and groups by generation, and for this reason the book should have been called *The Origin of Kinds*. To make this a little clearer, we need to speculate a little further about the art of classification.

"Class" and "classify" come from *classis*, meaning a "calling," "that which is called or summoned." For example, citizens are called for assessment, and young men are called up for military service, so, in the latter case, "the class of '52." Since the callings of men divided them into superior and inferior groups, the adjective *classicus* came to stand for the first or superior class; and hence, by an extension, "classic times" and "literary classic."

Incidentally, "class" and "clear" are related. "Clear" is from *clarus*, "clear, loud distinct sounds;" and *clarus* and *classis* derive from *clueo*, "to hear one's self called or named."

Man "calls up" classes in accordance with his needs. In Emerson's words, "Man animates all he can and sees all that he animates." His classifying and sorting and labeling ·his communal activities and the activities of nature have given him his different arts and sciences.

If every event were utterly unlike every other event, this would be impossible. Fortunately, the acts of nature, as well as those of men, follow the line of least resistance and, consequently, like the acts of men, develop habits of behavior. Nature repeats herself and thereby establishes certain regularities that men can name and label.

Every star, every tree, every snow-flake, every event *is* unique, but each also has some similarity to others of its kind which men can discern either by superficial or exact examination, "exact examination" being, by the way, an example of redundancy that the reader may ascertain for himself. By comparing shapes men can sort things out into sorts.

Sorting them by shape or arrangement of parts is one kind of sorting. This is *called* "classification by structure." A second kind of categorizing (ΚΑΤΆ, down, plus the root of 'ΑGΟRΕΎΟ, to speak in the market place, 'ΑGΟRΆ) , harangue, assert, or cataloguing (ΚΑΤΆ plus LÉGO, to lay in order) is on the basis of a common origin. And a third is on the basis of acting in a similar manner, that is, performing the same function (*functio* means a performing!)

Morphology, we know, is the study of forms. "Taxonomy" is the science of sorting them. The word is a compound of two Greek words. The verb ΤΆSSO means to arrange, to put in order, and the noun ΤΆXIS is an arranging, a drawing up in order, of soldiers. The second half comes from NOMÍA, distribution, NÓMOS being anything assigned or apportioned, a word that enters into many names of the sciences like "astronomy," "economy," and "agronomy."

A great many of our type-names or labels bear witness to the fact that mankind have been interested in the origin of species long before Darwin. "Kind" is akin to "kin," to *genus*, and to GÉNOS, all coming from an Ayran root meaning to produce or beget (compare "genesis" and "generate"). Hence all of these words have the meaning of sharing in a common descent and belonging to the same family. "Clan" is a Gaelic word that expresses the same idea.

"General" is a kindred word. It comes from *generalis*, of or belonging to a kind or species, of, or pertaining to, all. To generalize, which is supposed to be the philosophical activity *par excellence*, is, strictly, to find the likenesses of things in accordance with their *gens*, genus, genesis.

To these type-names of birth and descent must be added *natura* and *nascor* and their Greek equivalents, PHÝSIS and PHÝO. PHÝO means to bring forth, produce, to grow, get, beget, or generate, and PHÝSIS is the inborn quality or nature of a person or thing. *Nascor* is the equivalent verb in Latin, and *natura* the equivalent noun. A generation ago the science of *physics* was called *natural* philosophy. The nature of a thing (human nature—how many different meanings and how much babble this word has caused!) is what a thing is by birth, by generation—forgive me!—by nature. From PHÝLON, meaning a stock, race, or kind is derived the scientific term "phylum," used in biology to designate a major class by evolution.

When Shakespeare wrote, "One touch of nature makes

the whole world kin," he wrote something both more obvious and more profound than he fully realized—if we can trust Ben Jonson's report that Shakespeare knew little Latin and less Greek. The obvious point is that, of course, kind and nature are kin! Nature or PHÝSIS is the begetter of all the kin of this world of ours; and it is unreasonable that though all are kin, we treat some as kith, and worse still, some as aliens.

For a glib talker, there is nothing easier than generalization. He can sweep up all sorts of dissimilars into one grand category of his ad lib making. For a scientist striving to be a careful taxonomist, there is nothing more difficult. Give a graduate student in biology a bag of unclassified specimens gathered at the head-waters of the Orinoco. He has his dissertation right there, and it may take him months or years to determine whether some of these creatures are lizards or snakes.

It has taken centuries for biologists to arrive at their present system of classification of kindred. Some things that look alike got the label "spider." Some other things that look alike got the label "barnacle." Then more careful examination of the appearances called structure and origin led to putting spiders, barnacles, crabs, centipedes, grasshoppers, honey-bees, and an estimated million other species, to say nothing of individuals and their variations, under one sort and label it *arthropoda* ('ÁRTHRON, joint; PODÓS, foot). For, in truth, *arthropoda* is a phylum, since all of these creatures share a common origin and descent and deserve the same label for the same reason that all the MacGregors wear the same tartan, another kind of label or emblem.

Similar acts of behavior are given the same label. Slow acts of locomotion get the label "walk;" fast acts of locomotion get the label "run." From such movements come also all of our little but tremendously important words of relation, many of which are tied to the nouns and verbs themselves. We say he fell *down,* but we also say he had a *downfall;* or he was brought *up* well, and his *up*bringing was good. Also we get the separate labels "up," "down," "around," "after," and so forth.

Men's social performings or functions also get labeled. Running a household first gets the label "economy" from οικονομία, which is compounded of 'οîκος house and νέμο, to deal out, distribute, manage, control; and then the word is used to label a field of scientific study.

Sameness of shape in natural objects enabled men to develop their first science, geometry (GÊ, earth, and μετρέο, measure). And this science applied to the sameness of functioning of the heavenly bodies enabled them to arrive at the first natural science, astronomy. "Earth-measuring" applied to the heavenly bodies became "star-ordering" ('ASTÉR, star, and νέμο).

Undoubtedly, the last science of all will be a science of man, because though men do form individual and social habits, they are also extremely complex, erratic, and undependable. Man, the maker of sciences, is himself the worst possible material for a science.

It is a philosophical axiom that there can be no science of the individual, and this is rather obvious since every science is an attempt to order and label a group of individuals or things. But it is not true that you cannot know the individual, as some philosophers have averred. In medical research anomalies are always appearing, and the first time an anomaly appears it can be labeled and described. If it continues to appear, as is not unlikely, once a researcher has seen a single case, then the label for a unique case becomes the label of many, and a new class is formed.

Naming, classing, and labeling can cause much harm if they involve the misreading of appearances. There is only *one* human race, but uninformed persons speak as though there were white, brown, yellow, copper, and black races. This is a completely false classification based upon the superficial appearance of pigmentation. A much sounder classification of mankind is that based on blood types, but bloodtypes, to the consternation and confutation of the racist, cut across pigment types!

The universe like Gaul may be divided into three parts, and these together constitute all there is. There are the shapes and doings in the external world; there are their impressions on our sense organs, nerves, and brains; and there are names or symbols to "call out" and "point out" the first two.

Since shapes and doings are also signs and likewise their impresses on us, it can be said that man reads the natural signs and the reflected signs and orders them by artificial signs.

Is the Cosmos all form and no matter, all sign and no wax, all smoke and no fire? This was Plato's idea, if we discount some obscure remarks of his about space.

Though all reality may be mere appearances, phenomena—a magic lantern show of forms without substance—we still think that when we want to behold anything in its true light, we must come to grips with it.

And what do we seize hold of—form or substance? Substance, of course! So let us turn to it and see how substantial it is.

Chapter 6

SUBSTANCE

Anybody would just naturally assume that you would not have to look far to find matter—material things. There are shapes or forms and ideas, but there is also matter. Common sense would tell anybody that!

We must stop right there. Common sense (*sensus communis*) is, or was, the inner sense that was supposed to fuse all the incoming impressions from the several senses and thereby enable us to identify the feel, the taste, the smell, the warmth, and the form of a single object, say an orange. The common sense unites all of these *sensus* and makes it possible for us to say "orange," a symbol pointing to all of these *sensus* that adhere to one object or, rather, as we shall see in a moment, to one subject.

So in the technical language of the schools common sense, if it reports anything, reports that an orange is just a bundle of data. *Do, dare, dedi, datum*—do you recall that much Latin?—means to give. A datum is something given, a gift. The thing, orange, gives us a bundle of impressions, images, pictures, forms. Touch it, smell it, taste it, behold it, eat it—nothing but a nexus (a fastening together) of forms.

If we try to be conciliatory and accept the usual meaning of the term "common sense," namely the thinking and opining of normal, average, unsophisticated people, we must still raise an objection. To many who make "common sense" their criterion of sound thinking, the world is flat and women are obviously men's mental inferiors. This kind of person so frequently pounds the table or kicks the curbstone and says, "This is what I mean by matter."

Though we may have no quarrel with what he is trying to say nor, ultimately, with his form of demonstration, we must object to its brevity and to the ease with which he disposes of such weighty matters.

The truth of the matter is that we are confronted with a great paradox. The matter that we are all aware of, the matter of both common sense and science, is the most difficult thing to lay hold of. The consequence is that this chapter and the one to follow on "reality" may seem excessively metaphysical; but it cannot be helped, for matter and reality, upon careful examination, turn out to be the most elusive things in the whole world.

Before Plato had dissolved the world into forms that danced and flickered on the backdrop of space, the early Greek nature philosophers had said that everything was composed of earth, water, air, and fire. And this is still an unchallengeable assertion, if a rather crude one. A little later the Greeks Leucippus and Democritus refined this by attempting to go behind appearances.

Leucippus and Democritus did some hypothesizing, which derived from 'υπό, under, and θέσις, placing, means literally the same thing as its Latin cousin "suppose" (*sub,* under, and *pono,* to place). A hypothesis is a supposition, an underpining, a foundation on which to build. "Let us suppose for the sake of argument," someone says, and in so speaking, he is about to establish a hypothesis.

Leucippus and Democritus hypothesized that everything was composed of atoms. These ultimate bits of stuff ('Átomas, uncut, indivisible, from the privative prefix a and tomé, a cut) were the eternal units of reality. Their unions and separations in various proportions made everything on and under the sun. The hypothesis proved to be a fruitful supposition, but it had to wait twenty-four hundred years to come to fruition in the atomic theory of modern chemistry.

In the meantime Plato and Aristotle between them largely determined the course of philosophy and science for nearly two thousand years (say, from 400 B.C., to A.D. 1450). Though Plato knew the atomic hypothesis, he ignored it completely; and Aristotle rejected it in favor of his own "stuff."

The "stuff" that Aristotle hypothesized was tò 'upokeímenon, "the underlying" ('upó, under, and a participial form of the verb keímai, to lie). The Latin students of Aristotle, instead of borrowing this word, substituted one that means about the same thing—sub-jectum, a compound of sub, under, and jacio, to throw, cast.

Tò 'upokeímenon or the subjectum, which becomes, of course, our "subject," meant for Aristotle and his Latin followers three things: 1) the material out of which things are made, 2) the subject of attributes (an orange is the subject of all the attributes that our senses report), and 3) the subject of predicates.

Let us keep our eye chiefly on Number 1, noticing incidentally one of the interesting reversals in philosophy and philology. Aristotle meant by subject what we mean by object! A subject is the "stuff" to which attributes adhere or accidents inhere. This thing to which I point, *this* table, "has" a number of attributes which are incidental to it—its particular color, kind of wood, finish, design, dimensions, and age. All of these could be changed and will change with time, but the table is still a *subjectum*, something that rests under all of these accidents, which, from the verb *accido*, to fall, to happen, to chance, are really happenstances.

A subject can be an object, a "real thing," a substance (*substo*, to stand beneath) or it can be a grammatical substance, that is, a "substantive" about which things are predicated *(prae-dico, to cry in public, proclaim, preach, declare)*.

> *This* table is an antique.
> A table is a convenience for writing.

In the first example reference is to a substantial table; in the second to a substantive table (any table), but both, in the language of philosophy, are subjects and substantives. The first kind of substance—a "real" substance—which we can point to and make assertions about, Aristotle called a "first substance," and this is still, despite the attention we have given to grammatical substances, the matter that we are trying to lay hold of with both hands.

A man of substance—one who has a substantial income—is very much interested in substance, though for other reasons than the philosopher is. The Latin *substantia*, like our English word, also has these closely associated meanings: property, wealth, goods, effects, substance. The Greek 'υπόστασις also has these meanings, but—and here we encounter a complication that must be examined later—the Greek word which the Latins called "substance" was 'ουσία, a participle of 'ειμί, the verb to be.

The definition of 'ουσία is substantially that of the Latin *substantia*: that which is one's own, one's property, substance; the being, substance, essence of a thing. Thus the Greeks had a word for it that combines the most earthly things and the most etherial thing—being. This being so, it is not difficult to see why 'ουσία has been a substantial source of confusion for philogists, philosophers, theologians, and hard-working translators.

For centuries an iota's difference rent Christendom, making countless martyrs for both sides, there being all the difference in the world between the impressions of a HOMOIOUSIAN concerning the Three Persons of the Trinity and those of a HOMOOUSIAN, for the former held and holds (they are still with us under other names, having learned finally to live and let live) that the Persons of the Trinity are "like substance" ('όμοιος, like, and 'ουσία, substance), whereas the latter held and holds that They are the "same substance" ('όμος, same, and 'ουσία, substance).

Aristotle's "first substance," that which underlies all the appearances or phenomena of existence is 'ΰLE, which becomes the technical English prefix "hylo-." 'ULE means wood, forest, woodland, and, by an extension, firewood, logs of wood, and timber and by a further extension the material or stuff out of which anything is made, shaped, or formed. Like the Greeks we speak of the material for a coat or a play, and like Aristotle we also speak of the matter of the universe.

Aristotle's matter was, generally, the timber or stuff out of which anything is made: the timber of a ship, the stuff for a coat, or the material of a house, a play, a sentence, or a logical demonstration. Aristotle's "first matter" was a little closer to the matter of modern

33

science, the stuff of the universe, whether conceived as atoms or electrons.

The mass has nothing to do with mass, etymologically or otherwise, but the issue of substance is as crucial to Roman Catholic orthodoxy as it is to scientific orthodoxy. Without the hypothesis of substance, there can be no rational explanation of the mystery of Transubstantiation, when the accidents remain the same but the substance changes from bread to flesh.

For philosophic and scientific materialists matter is the matrix of everything, and the dissolution of nineteenth-century atoms into twentieth-century electrons arouses no dismay in their hearts. As one modern materialist sagely observed, no matter how thin you slice it, it is still matter.

The best refutation of the anti-materialist (or better still if it were not so awkward, anti-substancist) is language itself—whether English, Latin, or Greek. They all bear witness to the fact that the human mind finds matter a necessary term of our thinking. There are no Cheshire grins for the same reason that there are no Cheshire cats: shape or form that is the shape or form of nothing is a manifest absurdity.

Chapter 7

REALITY

Granted that "matter" or "substance" is a necessary term of our thinking, the question remains whether the "matter" of the universe is any more real than the "matter" of a book, the "matter" of "a public matter," or the "matter" of a syllogism. Rephrased the question is: Does Aristotle's prime matter or the matter of the scientific materialist *actually exist?* Is matter *actually real?*

Of all questions in philosophy this is the sixty-four dollar question, involving, as it does, the things that be and how we can know them and distinguish among them. The branch of philosophy that deals with the things that be, ΤΆ 'ΌΝΤΑ, is quite appropriately called, "ontology;" and the branch that deals with how we can know them is "epistemology," a compound of 'EPISTÉME, understanding, and LÓGOS.

Before we can attempt an answer to our question, we had better take a careful look at the words "real" and "exist," which we are in danger of assuming that we *really* know when we use them.

The difficulties that beset us in our previous effort to find something really substantial in a world of forms is vexingly illustrated by "thing" and "real," the two words that always land on the tip of our tongues when we want to draw a distinction between "reality" and "appearance."

"Real" is derived from *res* and is akin to 'RÉO, both of which are defined as that which is said or spoken,

'RÉO being the root of some forms of a verb, to ask, and of another, to speak. It is not surprising then that *res* comes to mean most any thing. It means, among other things, a thing, matter, affair, event, an actual thing. It also means a business affair and a law case. *Res publica* means things of public concern and, hence, the commonweal, commonwealth, republic.

Now look at "thing." An Old English "Thing" was a meeting, especially a judicial assembly, and in Scandanavian countries a "Ting" is a parliament. Other meanings similar to those of *res* accrued, and among these are a law suit, a deed, event, a statement, a thought, an actual being as opposed to a symbol of it, and a material substance. In law a thing that can be possessed is distinguished from a person.

Consequently, both "real" and "thing," by which we try to mean something substantial and enduring, not only derive much of their significance from the activities of political gatherings where so much hot air is released, but signify almost any kind of event from an opinion to something substantial that may be talked about. The expression, "the real thing" means, etymologically speaking, "the thingy thing" or "the really real."

So there is no doubt that matter is a "real thing," but so is Mr. Jones's meterological observation, "Nice day!" It, therefore, becomes apparent that we shall have to discriminate among "real things."

Can we say that matter exists and Mr. Jones's ephemeral "nice day!" does not?

"Exist" and the Medieval Latin *existentia* derive from the preposition *ex* and the verb *sto,* to stand; so the compound means to stand out, to stand forth, and, hence, to be visible, to exist, to be. To exist is to have "real being" as contrasted to "imaginary being."

But what is it to be? And what is the difference between "being" and "existence?"

The Latin *sum,* I am, has a number of obsolete subjunctive forms that reveal its relation to ΡΗΎΟ, which, as we know, means to bring forth, produce, to be born, to be by nature (ΡΗΎΣΙΣ *is* nature), to be. So etymologically there is no difference between "being" and "existing," and, if anything, "being" has priority in the sense of being by nature, being born into this world.

It was Aristotle and his medieval followers who made the distinction, making "being" the genus and "existence" the species. All that we talk about, predicate, has being. Whatever we make a substantive has being. This tree is . . . Beauty is . . . Pegasus is . . . The dinosaur is . . . Santa Claus is . . . All of these have being, but only the first has existence.

The issues arising from making distinctions between being and existence are too many and too turbulent to explore further in a primer of this kind. They have divided philosophers into two camps down through the centuries, and the contemporary excitement over *existentialism* demonstrates that the main issue is still very, very much in evidence, and on the Left Bank, at least, may result in an issue of blood.

We can now attempt an answer to our initial question. Matter has being, along with everything else, but has it existence? The man of common sense and the scientific materialist give a vigorous affirmative sign. Aristotle and his celebrated Christian follower, Thomas à Quinas, give a much more qualified assent.

37

Matter, 'ÚLE, the stuff of things, has potential existence! Being the potentiality of every existing thing, it must have some sort of quasi-existence, something more than non-being; but it does not *as* matter have actual (being in act) existence.

All the things of our experience are shaped matter, that is, informed matter, a union of matter and form. We never, no matter where we look, in the heavens above or on the earth beneath, perceive matter bare, as Edna Millay's Euclid looked on pure, dross-free forms.

Then how do we know that there is such a thing? We must hypothesize such a potential stuff half way between non-being or nothingness and actual being.

The cloth is the stuff of a coat, the wool is the stuff of the cloth, the hairs of the sheep are the stuff of the wool . . . Everything is the material of something else, but hypothetically there must be pure potentiality without actual form. So says the hylomorphism ('ÚLE, material, and MORPHÉ, form) of both Aristotle and Thomas.

We take a piece of paper and roll it into the shape of a cone. It now has an existence of some kind. Did it exist before I rolled it up? A deceptively simple question with a hundred different answers, but let us listen only to Aristotle, who listened attentively to what the Greek language was saying. Yes, it had some sort of existence. The paper was the potentiality, the matter, that then became a cone. As an actual cone it is an entity (*ens* from *esse,* to be; compare "absence"; *abs + ens*). It is, in the language of Aristotle, a vertible first substance PRÓTE 'OUSÍA) compounded of matter ('ÚLE) and form (MORPHÉ).

Prior to its being shaped into a cone, it was just a piece of paper. However, as paper it was an entity composed of matter (the potential stuff being wood pulp) with a "determinate" form. We point to it and say, "This is paper." And if anyone asks us what paper is, we "define" it.

Since "define" comes from *de* + *finio,* to finish, and "determinate" from de + *termino,* to set bounds to, to limit, to define a thing is to state its determinate form. When we do this we get at a thing's "essence."

Now "essence" is derived from *esse,* to be; and means the same thing as that elusive little word 'ousía. And 'ousía, we know, is also translated as "substance." The Greek equivalent of "substance" is 'upóstasis. In Christian theology 'upóstasis is also translated as "person." The three persons of the Trinity are also three Hypostases or three Ousias. *Hence!* "essence" also has these overtones of meaning. "Essence," 'ousía, 'upóstasis, "substance," and "subject" are all semantic siblings; and the would-be philosopher may tear his hair at having to do with such elusive shapes, but grapple with them he must, for they are the core of speech and thought.

How do we determine a thing's essence? By discovering its purpose, its end. We define by stating a thing's *finis*—what it aims to be. And what it aims to be is what it does. Define "pencil," "stomach of an animal," "plant," "man," "person of the Trinity," and you define its "nature," "essence," "end," or "function."

"Function," a new term, comes from *fungor,* to be busy, to engage in, to perform, to execute; and then comes to mean in English, in addition to these meanings, the kind of action proper to anything by which it fulfills its purpose.

In accordance with ancient ways of viewing things, the breath is the life, and the life is the moving principle of the body. A plant, an animal, and a man have life. What is the difference? To define the difference is to point out the difference of function, the difference of operation (*opera,* work, labor), the difference of working.

The breath that is the life is also the soul of things. The soul or ghost (German *geist*) is akin to *anima, spiritus,* PSÝCHE, and PNEÛMA, all of which meant "breath." *Spiro,* from whence "inspiration," "perspiration," "respiration," and "spirit," means to breathe and to blow, and so do PSÝCHO and PNÉO. *Anima* can be recognized in "animal," "animate," and "anemone," the wind-flower. From PNEÛMA we got both "pneumonia" and "pneumatic;" and from PSÝCHE, "psyche," "psychic," and "psychology."

From the foregoing it will not be too difficult to understand what Aristotle meant when he defined the soul, the psyche, as the "entelechy" of the body. Aristotle coined this word from 'EN in, TÉLOS, end, and 'ÉCHO, have—in other words, that which has its end in itself. In other words that have little to do with ghostly mysteries, the soul is the function of the body. If the eye were an animal, Aristotle says in order to clarify his meaning, sight would have been its soul. Plants have a nutritive soul; animals, a nutritive and a sentient soul; and man, a nutritive, a sentient, and a rational soul.

We return to our question: what is real? Reality is a matter of levels, ranging from nothingness or non-being, through the potentiality of prime matter, to informed, ensouled, actual, functioning matter, Insofar as a thing functions well it is real. A healthy, flourishing plant has more reality than a sickly one that will never reach maturity and be what it is supposed to be both in act and in definition. A mature normal man has more reality, more fullness of being, than an infant, a child, or an idiot. A thinking man is more fully a man than one of muscles and mush.

"Perfection" derives from *perficio* (for *per + facio*), which means to make thoroughly, completely, to carry through, to finish. Every manufacturer (*manu,* hand, and *facere,* to make) should devote himself to finished products, manifesting their excellence, whether they be mouse-traps or his own person.

The perfection of man is to be a wise man, knowing himself. And this means knowing how to act, to function, most completely in keeping with his own individuality and in keeping with his humanity.

The perfection of society—one with the most fullness of being and, therefore, the most reality—is, as the name reveals (*socio,* to join or unite together, to hold in common, to share; *socius,* a fellow sharer, comrade, partner), each member working at that which he can do best and receiving his share, one sufficient to perfect his unique talent and his humanity.

CHAPTER 8

RETURN TO EARTH

The muscles with which we began this exploration have enabled us to climb into rarefied regions, if not the region of the blessed. But now, like Anteus, we need to renew our strength by returning to earth, to the muscles that intimately reveal to us the real nature of action, of energy, of force, and of matter in the sense of the "resisting other."

The touching, feeling sense is an active thing. We push gently or firmly against things and know that they are there. Sound falls upon ears and light falls upon eyes and make their impress on passive clay—or so it seems. Sound is a vibration of one kind of matter, air; and light is either waves in the ether or pellets (quanta) of something—energy or matter? But whatever light is, it is now established that it too feels the tug of gravity.

Our sense of reality comes ultimately from touch, and if we can trust the theories of the scientists, this owes most of its character to that great mystery called "gravity." Earth and star-bound things are real; aerial and etherial things less real; and the symbols made by men to label reality most unreal of all. And yet . . . a voice crying in the wilderness can move, to put it crassly, tons upon tons of human flesh century after century; and $E = mc^2$—what will this move before we have heard the last of it?

We reach out our hands and touch something in the dark. It resists. "This thing is real," touch says; and though our more sophisticated senses of hearing and vision, enamoured of the spoken and written symbols that they helped discover, half persuade us that "touch," and "matter" are only names, we still believe that the sense of touch is the touchstone of reality. The eyes may see mirages and the ears hear disembodied voices, but the muscles and their attendant genius, touch, can infallibly distinguish between nothing and something.

So let us acknowledge the superior wisdom of naive realists who refute Plato and Berkeley and other formalists by kicking curbstones and let us accept their demonstration as the final word.

This body, this SÔMA, this corpus (alas! so soon to be a corpse), this carnal being that feasts on flesh like other *carnivora* and will become a cadaver, because it will fall down dead (*cado,* to fall down), this union of psyche and soma subject of and to psycho-somatic ills—this, however great the illusion, is what we know most intimately. And touch, however far we may soar on the wings of light and sight and name and classify things in terms of our purposes, our ends, and speak so confidentally of the "essence" of things, tells us more about the essence of things than the corpus of Aristotle and of Thomas fused in a perfect corporation of signs and symbols.

It is through the appetite and the modifications of touch called taste and smell that we know the object of our desire. It is through pain, the tearing touch, that we know both our own matter and that of the hostile other. It is through work, wrestling with the inchoate, that we know indeed that matter exists to be formed

43

and come to respect and admire its stubborn resistence to our design. It is to be the mother of something that we know our creator or, more correctly, our creatrix.

And finally it is through the touching explorations of love that we know both our love and the beloved. Mystery comes from the verb ΜΫΟ, to have the lips or eyes closed. And, truly, in the mystery of love both lips and eyes are closed so that not speaking we may hear and not seeing we may see.

It is to the earth we go for renewal, both the sower of seed and the city-dweller on a holiday. In Greek earth is GÊ, and the goddess of the earth is Gaea, the mother of all things, the counsellor of earth and men, and the origin of the oracles of both Delphi and Olympia. *Terra firma* we know as a cliché, but not *Tellus,* akin to terra and meaning the same thing. And Tellus was the Roman Gaea.

And this brings us to another great mystery that only the Genius of the Latin tongue could reveal. This is the remarkable kinship of *materia,* matter, *mater,* mother, and *matrix,* womb.

Is it only chance that the tongue of the Romans should offer such striking testimony on behalf of the Great Mother of Ancient Culture. Certainly, Latin says quite clearly: matter is the mother from whose matrix all things, living and non-living, issue forth into the light of the sun and become visible forms.

And certainly all hylozoists ('ÚLE, matter, and ZOÉ, life) and all hylomorphists would have to agree, at least, that it is a matter for serious thought, though the hylozoists be out-and-out materialists and the hylomorphists be followers of St. Thomas.

CHAPTER 9

TWISTS OF THE TONGUE

A teacher of a foreign language can put his pupil's hands on a book and say, "Book." The pupil then says, "Book." Thereupon they both nod vigorously, delighted with such complete sensuous and verbal communion.

In the language of the current concern about language called semantics, the referent, the book; the symbol, "book;" and the thought, impression, or engram in each brain are all rather intimately and clearly related. And though communication at this level is not infallible by any means, as that continuous state of misunderstanding named "marriage" demonstrates, communication continues to be a going concern as long as words serve as labels for physical things—plants, bench marks, or light streaks on photographic plates—and, much less dependably, for human things—the viscera of the body, family life, and national life. And the remarkable progress in the arts and sciences for the last three hundred years shows what can be done when symbols have clear referents, either physical things or physical operations on things.

But when abstraction (*abstraho,* to draw away, detach) increases, and certain general words become so commonly used that everyone takes it for granted that the referents are clear—big words like "Beauty," "Truth," "Love," "Justice," and "Freedom," we may make the error of children and primitives and assume that these big substantives have the same kind of reality as the substance named "tree" or "book," the "first substances" of Aristotle. The making of such general terms into first substances is called reification *(res,* thing).

The philosopher, if he is also a wise man, knows that language is a tool to label, order, and share human experience; and conscious of all the difficulties, he is inclined to taciturnity *(taceo,* to be silent, to hold one's peace). The sophist considers it a tool to serve his own ulterior ends; and the fool *(follis,* a bellows or wind-bag), enchanted by his own lubricious tongue wants, not an auditor, but a sounding board.

The improper use of words, of which careless abstraction and reification are flagrant examples, is responsible for some of the confusion of tongues, but most of the difficulty is due to the necessity of using symbols that originally pointed to the sensuous world of physical things to deal with our private world of impressions that physical things have made on us. The words that pertained originally to our bodies and their encounters with the stuff of this world must also serve to designate the operations of our inner life.

Man, for better or for worse, is an incorrigible materialist, and nothing proves that more irrefutably than the languages of mankind. Only one example need be adduced *(adduco,* to bring forward), namely, *spiro,* the physical act of breathing, which has inspired such spiritual substances as *spiritus,* the good spirits of the man who has just dined well, alcoholic spirits, the Time Spirit, and the Holy Spirit.

This inescapable condition of being human and functioning all the time on two levels has necessitated a kind of duplicity that has nothing to do with intentional two-timing. Only by ingenious twists of the tongue that have all the characteristics of "double-talk" has man been able to do justice to the duality inherent in outer and inner life.

The word "trope" (TRÓPOS, a turning) is mostly encountered in scientific terms implying the simplest reactions of living creatures. Moths are phototropic (PHÔS, light) and the sunflower and other heliotropes are heliotropic ('ÉLIOS, the sun). The word "trope" is also the general name in books of rhetoric for figures of speech, that is, turns of speech, or more literally still (oddly, "literally" really means "materially"), as the title of this chapter has it, twists of the tongue.

Now it is a common error to think that only poets are concerned with figures of speech. Actually, every day of our lives, every time that we give tongue to our thoughts, we are making turns of speech, as the sequel will prove.

The two main forms of speech are, of course, prose and poetry. And here immediately we encounter paradox. Prose, as one of the turns of speech, is, etymologically, the one that does not turn but goes right straight ahead. "Prose" is derived from the adjective *prosus,* which means straight forward, direct. In short, prose is prosaic because it does not have twists and turns like poetry.

By the twists of language it is thought that anybody can speak prose but that it takes talent to speak poetically. The paradoxical truth is that we speak poetically much of the time and prose rarely. In the evolution of language prose is always a later development than poetry.

Prose may be said to be trimmed and cropped poetry, and poetry, luxuriant prose, full of, to use a Johnsonian

47

substantive, sinuosities (*sinus,* a fold or bend) ; and we do not formulate these definitions with the intention of insinuating that one rather than the other deserves the olive crown. However, it is still true that good prose is a rarer thing than poetry, good and bad.

The good poet has a *penchant* for seeing similarity in dissimilarity and is always minting a coin called a "simile," one image in some one fitting respect being like another. Smoke and fire, falling leaves as the harbinger of winter and death, the vernal equinox and resurrection, scales and justice, wigs and jurists—the poet sees them first, then makes us see them, and then they become a part of our living heritage. And by poet we do not just mean one who is a verse-writer by profession. We mean the seer and maker of original genius in every walk of life from tent-maker, carpenter, shipwright, and wheelwright to prophet and playwright.

When a comparison is not expressed by using "like" or "as" but is implied by shifting the meaning of a word used in one context to another, the turn of speech is termed a "metaphor," METAPHORÁ, which comes from the verb METAPHÉRO (METÁ, over, and PHÉRO, carry, that is, *transfer* or *translate*). A simple example is:

The ship *plows* the sea.

In our tongue the master-builder of metaphor was Shakespeare.

Very close to metaphor in etymology and meaning is "metonymy," compounded of the same preposition and 'ÓNOMA, name, which with three other prefixes also give us, "synonym," "antonym," and homonym." "Metonymy" is a trope in which an attribute represents the thing or the thing signified, a double metonym that is usually cited being "The pen is mightier than the sword."

Another close relative is "synecdoche," from a complicated Greek word that we need not bother to analyze. It literally means to take or receive with something else, which throws little light on its technical meaning. In "synecdoche" a more comprehensive term is used for a less comprehensive one, a whole for a part, or a genus for a species, or, in each of these three cases, the reverse. Examples are "Give me ten right-arms;" "I'll have a drop;" "Who is this creature?" "A Word to the Reader."

Then there is "onomatopoeia," which is better known because it is such a formidable looking term. It also is a misleading term in terms of its origin, for being compounded of 'ÓNOMA, name, and POIÉO, to make, it means name-making. Actually the term refers to only one kind of name-making—words that sound like the thing signified, like "hiss" and "buzz." "Bomb" comes to us by way of Italian and Latin from the Greek BÓMBOS, any deep hollow sound. An English-speaking child would have given us the word anyway, for clearly a bomb is a "boom-boom."

A long, sustained metaphor is called a "parable," (PARABOLÉ, a compound of PARÁ, beside, and BÁLLO, to throw or cast). Literally it means throwing or placing side by side. Akin to "parable" is "allegory," from 'ALLEGORÉO, to speak one thing and mean another, as its analysis reveals, for it is composed of 'ÁLLOS, other, and 'AGORÉUO, to speak in the market-place, the agora. A word compounded of the prefixes of these two words, PARÁ and 'ÁLLOS, is "parallel." And "parallel" is the key to the meaning of parable and allegory, as well as being the clue to understanding and writing them: saying one

49

thing and meaning the other, usually a literal (material) narrative with a parallel "symbolical" meaning.

In the parable of the sowers Jesus talked quite simply, as he always did, about the sower sowing seed upon the earth. His disciples, being literalists like so many million literalists that came afterwards, took him literally; whereas, as usual, he was speaking parabolically, allegorically, metaphorically.

The irony is that his followers then and now also speak every day of their lives in parable, allegory, and metaphor. It is true that not being prophets and makers themselves, they did and do so unwittingly. For the same reason they were content to repeat, without understanding, current phrases until they grew into clichés, stereotypes, and platitudes. It is also true that all of us, Christian and pagan, must, all the days of our lives, consciously or unconsciously, speak parabolically, allegorically, metaphorically . . . symbolically.

Let us take as a prosaic example the twists of the tongue that we are always giving our touchstone of reality: "touch."

1) He touched the stove and got burnt. (literal fact)
2) He touched the stove and got burnt. (brief parable or allegory)
3) Touch is an organ of the body.
4) He is touched. (emotionally moved)
5) He is touched. (crazy)
6) He is touched. (selected for membership in a fraternity)
7) He is touched. (asked for a contribution)
8) He (a traveler) touched many points.
9) He (a speaker) touched on many points.
10) He touched up the picture.

50

11) The tangent touches the circle. (Naturally! "Tangent" is from *tango,* to touch. The sentence says, "The circle-touching line touches the circle.")
12) The cloud is touched with rose.
13) He touched on blasphemy.
14) This touches my pride.
15) The jockey touched the horse.
16) It was touch and go.
17) *Touchée!*

Finally, let us scrutinize this remark that might have been made by one of the lowest denizens of the lowest pool hall: "The skirt touched me for a cup of Java; and like a dope I tossed her a deuce because her sob-story touched me." Aside from the two metaphorical uses of "touch," the remark includes a bad simile, and five metonyms, of which two are synecdoches.

If his auditor were a punster with a little more polish than the speaker, he would have had a compulsion to reply, "The deuce you say!"

Anyway, the exclamation should have been made at some point by the reader of this essay on semantics, which has been not only a tale of two worlds but a homily on evil. If we can trust the voice of mankind, twoness, duality, is everywhere the sign of evil, showing its face both in the deuce of dice and in the Greek prefix DYS-, and in the Latin and English prefix, *dis-, dis*ease being a common, and "dyslogistic" an uncommon, example.

Men struggle against a myriad forms of schizophrenia and strive for wholeness, oneness. Some try to achieve it by the monism of materialism; others by the monism of idealism. They think that by clinging to one horn of the dilemma, they can avoid the other. It is a delusion. To live is to be impaled on both horns.

Chapter 10

BY WAY OF ANALOGY

Poets—and the rest of us—use puns, similes, metaphors, allegories, and parables. Scientists try to avoid these giddy toys, these surprising twists of the tongue, and employ instead such things as reckonings, calculations, computations, ratios, proportions, and analogies. Yet an analysis of the meanings of these forms of operation discloses a closer consanguinity with the poet's figures than one taught to revere exact science and sneer at versifying would believe.

We must first look at the last of these operational forms of science, for being Greek it is the eldest both in time and significance. "Analogy" in the form "analogue" came into English meaning the same thing that it meant in Greek mathematics—a mathematical proportion or an agreement of ratios. But 'ΑΝΑΛΟΓΙΆ, composed of 'ΑΝΆ, up, up to, and ΛΌΓΟΣ, speech, thought, also meant what "analogy" means in English: likeness of one thing to another and is so close in meaning to metaphor that one dictionary gives "the *apple* of his eye" as an example of analogy. The Greek verb derived from 'ΑΝΑΛΟΓΙΆ means to count up, sum up, and calculate; and the substantative formed in turn from this verb means a counting up, a calculation.

In other words, 'ΑΝΑΛΟΓΙΆ and its verb are the Greek words that carry all the meanings of the Latin-derived words that are employed to define it—count, relate, compute, reckon, calculate, and their noun forms, and ratio and proportion. Since all of these are a part of every schoolboy's vocabulary, we think we know what we mean when we use them. But do we?

Ratio is to Latin what 'ANALOGIÁ is to Greek. *Ratio* means a reckoning, an account, a calculation, or computation and is derived from the verb *reor,* to reckon, calculate, which, it seems, comes from a root that is akin to *res,* thing. So in general 'ANALOGIÁ is *ratio* and *ratio* is 'ANALOGIÁ; and it is correct to say that one is the translation of the other if we do not forget that translation is a metaphorical operation.

And what is it "to reckon?" Why "to count" and "to relate." And what is it "to calculate?" Why to lay pebbles in order *in order* to keep a tally. The *calculus* was a pebble used in voting for or against an accused person in court, a black pebble (now it's a black *ball*) meaning condemnation, a white one, acquittal. Such pebbles were also used to reckon accounts. And finally, what is it "to relate?" In English, as in Latin, it is to recount or narrate, to connect, to establish some kinship between things.

But this is what "metaphor," "parable," and "allegory" do. So if we are not back where we started from, we are not so far away. "Metaphor," "parable," "allegory," "analogy," "ratio," "reckon," "relate," "count," and "compute" (these two from *com-puto,* to trim, arrange, reckon) —all these words, along with our old friend "symbol," to throw together, are semantic siblings. All of them are names for what we do when two things more or less alike have some common denominator so that we can—to introduce one more term—"equate" them. "Equate" comes from *aequus,* a word of many meanings but all signifying uniformity of kind, nature, or rank. An *aequum* is a level spot, a plain; an *aequus* is a friend, one who is equitable and has respect for equity. "Equal," "equation," "equivocal," and "equivocate," so different in meaning, also trace their ancestry to *aequus. Proportio,* from whence "proportion," meant comparative relation, analogy, likeness; and the modern definition of proportion is "equality of ratios," the meaning of which is so elusive that mathematicians can quarrel over it far into the night.

MÁTHEMA is that which is learned, a lesson. It comes from an infinitive form of the verb MANTHÁNO, to learn by enquiry, to ascertain, to understand. The noun MATHETÉS means a learner or a pupil and is the equivalent of the Latin *discipulus,* a disciple. The plural of MÁTHEMA, with the appropriate form of the definite article, TÀ MATHÉMATA, was the Greek word for "mathematics," the most rigorous of scientific disciplines, that is, matters of instruction.

The poet has an eye to figures; the mathematician has an eye to figures. Thus we have made an equation, a ratio, and a metaphor. Also there is a metonymy here and, alas, punning and equivocation.

We have found the bond of kinship between the poet and the mathematician: both have a penchant for seeing relations or analogies. This one thing they have in common; in all other respects they are quite different; but this is the case with all good metaphors and with all good ratios.

The poet, unless somewhat restrained by Classicism, luxuriates in all the wealth of analogy that the sensuous world has to offer him. The mathematician limits himself chiefly to one kind of relation, quantity, and to forms denuded of individuality which matter contributes. The poet revels in the concrete; and when he writes, he loads his line with images that explode in the mind like a sky-rocket in the darkness. The mathematician is as sparing of overtones of association as an ascetic is of food. Poetry is concrete; mathematics is abstract.

We have already considered the metaphorical and analogical nature of all words dealing with our interior life, with mind, spirit, emotion, and thought. Let us now look at some examples of the process in reverse.

"Machine" comes from MECHANÉ, which is from the adjective, MÊCHOS, a means, an expedient, a contrivance, and the related verb, MECHANÁOMAI, means to make by art, put together, and construct. Hence a machine is a contrivance to achieve some end. A man can be a machine as much as one made by art. Slaves were the machines of Ancient Times and Times not so Ancient; and invented machines were to make us free men—an end that still seems far off.

An organic creature is usually considered the opposite of a mechanical creature, but this is not a very satisfactory antithesis. 'ORGANON means an instrument, tool, or engine and is derived from 'ÉRGON, work. A heart or a stomach is an organ, but so also is a battery or a carburetor. An organic creature is composed of interacting organs, but so also is a "creature" (product of a creator) like an automobile.

"Automobile," "automatic," and "automaton" get their "auto" from 'AUTÓS, meaning self, and 'AUTÓMATOS the adjective, means acting of one's own will, unbidden, self-moving—spontaneous, which derives from *sponte,* free will! Strictly speaking, of all things on the earth only man is an automaton, a self-moved being.

"Engine" is another interesting word that has also fallen into the bad company of machines. *Ingenium* is that which is inborn, innate, natural talent, an ingenious person, a genius. Both "engine" and "genius" derive from *genero,* to beget, create. An automobile or a train is *not* an "engine;" it is a machine, an instrument, a utensil, and, yes, an organ. Man, on the other hand, is *not* a machine, as some misinformed materialists argue; he *is* an engine, the most wonderful engine on earth, perhaps, in the universe.

Some of this shift in the meaning of terms has been, of course, due to careless borrowing by men of science, but there is a deeper explanation than this. "Reason," "rational," and "ratio" are blood brothers, as will become manifest in the next chapter; and the making of ratios and engaging in ratiocination is the process of discovering likenesses. Nothing, moreover, can be known, understood, by itself, but only in relation to something else and by analogy. A mechanical chess-player seems like a self-willed creature; *ergo,* an automaton. An instrument that seems to travel by its own innate powers— an *engine.*

What is a human being? Why he is something like a machine. What is a machine? Why it is something like a human being. What is God? Why something like a human being if he had perfected all of his potentialities and was pure function without earthly limitation. And what is a human being? A creature made in the image (likeness) of his Creator.

Chapter 11

REASON AND VISION

Just as there are two kinds of "seeing" of kinship, analogy, and ratio, so also there are two kinds of knowing: reason and intuition.

But first, what is it "to know?"

Sensation is thought to be a passive thing, but perception (*percipio*, to take wholly, to seize entirely) is an active seeing. We do not heed all of the sensations we are having at any one moment, but what we perceive we are aware of. Conception (*concipio*, to take with both hands, to take to one's self, to conceive) is a little stronger still. To "conceive" an idea bears some similarity to a woman's conceiving a child. We "perceive" various men, and then "conceive" the concept "man." In the seventeenth century a "concept" was a "conceit," but a "conceit" also meant a fanciful notion, and this is still its chief meaning.

When we "know" something, our minds "seize upon" it or "grasp" it, or we "understand" it, all of which, of course, are pure metaphors. English-speaking peoples "under-stand" something; the Greeks "over-stood" ('EΠΊ over; ΊSTEMI, stand) something. Also in imitation of the Romans we "apprehend" (*apprehendo, ad + prehendo*, grasp, seize . . . prehensile tail!) and "comprehend" (*com + prehendo*).

Someone remarks, "Why don't you get next to him" or "on to him," and the English idiom is clear. It should be equally clear that here again is metaphor.

57

The Greek 'οἶδα, which comes from the Indo-European root meaning "to see," means "to know." What I see I know. And English "know," Latin *nosco* (old form *gnosco*), and Greek ΓΙΓΝΌΣΚΟ, all meaning "to acquire knowledge of," "to become acquainted with," all come from the same root as "can." The original meaning of the present tense of "can" was "I have learned," that is, "know." Ben Jonson wrote, "She could the Bible in the holy tongue"—that is, she "knew" it.

The Old English "couth," which survives today in "uncouth," was the past participle of "cunnan," "can," and meant known, familiar, acquainted. The intimate relation between "can" and "know" may be seen quite clearly in the German *Kunst*, art, skill, dexterity. *Magister der frein Kunste* is "Master of the Liberal (Free) Arts," or the degree of M.A.

Thus "to know" is "to see" and "to be able." Also "to know" is to do mentally what the hands ("apprehend,") eyes ("see"), and body ("understand") do when they make dynamic contact with an object or maneuver around it. Only by living and dead metaphor is it possible to talk about the operations (workings) of the mind, which is the instrument of linking two things in the bond of kinship called analogy, ratio, metaphor, and symbol.

Quite appropriately *nosco* and *gnosco*, which gives us "know," also gives us "gnostic," "cognoscente," and "connoisseur." However, the last two gentlemen, aesthetic devotees of the senses, would not bother to take cognizance of the first or recognize him on the street because of his knowledge of things known only to those with second sight.

58

"Reason" is one way of knowing. Its origin is seen more obviously in the longer synonym, "ratiocination." "Reason" derives from the same source as *ratio*—from the verb *reor*, which, as we have seen, is related to *res*, thing, and which designates as vague a mental operation as English "think," for it means to reckon, calculate, believe, think, imagine, suppose, and so on. English "reason," like "ratiocinate" and *ratiocinatio*, is a much more specific operation than *reor*. The Greek semantic equivalent is SYLLOGÍSOMAI, a verb compounded of the Greek preposition for "with" (SYL- is a combining form of SYN-) and our old elusive friend LÓGOS, and means to sum up or reckon up.

Our "syllogism" comes straight from the Greek noun derived from this verb, and its closest English equivalent is probably, ignoring later usage, "computation" (*con*, a combining form of *cum*, with, and *puto*, to reckon, count, think). The Greek verb LÉGO, from whence LÓGOS, "logical," and "syllogism," and the Latin *puto* reveal interesting variations in their semantic evolution from names for physical acts to names for mental acts. LÉGO meant "to lay in order" and then, by extension, "to speak," "to reckon," and then in SYLLOGÍSOMAI, to infer. *Puto*, originally meaning "to purify," came to mean "to prune or trim trees," "to arrange," "to reckon," "to count," "to think." At the heart of both words is the idea of putting things in order.

The adjective LOGIKÓS means belonging or pertaining to either speech or reason, and, in the second sense, "fit for reasoning." 'E LOGIKÉ is elliptical for 'E LOGIKÉ TÉCHNE, the art of reasoning or logic.

The syllogism is the chief figure of formal logic. In a syllogism two propositions or premises are put forth, and from them can be inferred a conclusion. "Infer" and "inference" comes from *infero* (*in* plus *fero*, to bear and carry), which means, among many things, to bring forward, to produce, to conclude; and "conclude" comes from *con-cludo*, to shut up, confine, bring to an end, infer. So though a conclusion is an inference and an inference is a conclusion, it is also true that an inference leads to a conclusion!

Study of a syllogism like the following example reveals that it is always composed of three terms, one of which is a middle term ("animal" in this example); and "syllogism" is, in practice, really the name for mediate (*medius*, middle) inference. Reasoning by means

> Animal is substance
> Man is animal
> ———————————
> Man is substance

(*medius*, middle!) of a middle term is also called "discursive reason," literally, running to and fro (*discurro*), but, technically, moving indirectly from premise to conclusion.

There are supposed to be two kinds of discursive reasoning: inductive (*inductio*, a leading or bringing into), which starts with data and arrives at a general truth, and deductive (*deductio*, a leading off), which starts with a general truth or two such truths and moves to another, as in the syllogism. The scientist is supposed to employ inductive reasoning and the "arm-chair" philosopher deductive reasoning, but actually they are so intimately related that one is dependent upon the other.

The opposite of discursive reasoning is "insight"—a direct seeing into the truth of things without ratiocination. The Latin-derived equivalent is "intuition" from *in* and *tueor,* to look at, gaze at, behold. It is intuition rather than reason that gives one vision (*video,* to see) and wisdom, ultimately from the same root from which both "to see" and "to know" are derived.

A man of reason, a rational man, can be absolutely brilliant in his reasoning and yet lack both common sense and wisdom. On the other hand, the intuitive man, piercing to the heart of things with a *coup d'oeil* and beholding similitude everywhere, may be too prone to reckless conjecture (*conjecto,* to throw together, surmise, guess) and speculation (*specio,* to look at, behold), that is, viewing things for their own sake with a speculative mind rather than pragmatically as a stockmarket speculator does.

Both the scientist and the visionary theorize, which, along with theatre, comes from ΤΗΕΆΟΜΑΙ, to view, gaze at, behold; and both, of course, may possess equal intelligence despite the contrast in their ways of seeing and dealing with similies and ratios.

In a period that has so much misplaced faith in intelligence tests, it is wise to take a second look at this word "intelligence." It derives from *intelligens,* which is a participial form of *intelligo,* which, in turn, is compounded of *inter,* between, among, and *lego,* which, like its kinsman ΛΈΓΟ is a verb of many meanings, to lay or put together, to collect, pick out, select, choose, to read aloud, to call out.

Nothing in the whole world is more fascinating than these inter-relations, these kinships, these analogies, these ratios between these two words ΛΈΓΟ and *lego* and their offspring and between all of these words and the operations that they designate. Logos, logic, analogical, syllogism, dialectic (DIÁ, through, by means of, and LÉGO) and intellect, intelligence, and legal are some of them.

What *is* "intelligence?" Why it is the ability, potential or actual, to intellectualize. The Latin equivalent is *intelligo,* an inflectional disguise for *inter-lego*. Is it surprising, then, that "to *inter-lego*" is "to DIA-LÉGO?" And what is it "to DIA-LÉGO?" Why at its lowest level it is to lay sounds in order, that is, to speak. It is also to speak a local form of language, that is, to speak dialect, and it is, highest of all, to dialecticize. In the history of philosophy dialectic is the kind of conversation (dialogue) that Socrates had with his pupils in order, through such an exchange of opinions, to arrive at the truth. Dialectic then came to mean the logic of disputation, but to limit it to this kind of thinking would be a grave error.

Hegel, by turning his back on the arid formal logic of Scholasticism, returned at a higher level of performance, to the dialectical methods of Plato. Dialectic, as it was employed by Plato and Hegel, and therefore, in its best and broadest sense, is the process of discovering and uncovering the similarities and contradictions inherent in things, terms, and notions by the free play of both insight and reason.

Chapter 12

DOING THINGS

The little substantive "act" and the littler verb "do" are probably the commonest words in the language for . . . what? If we follow a widely used dictionary and say that "act" is "that which is done" and that "do" is "to bring about," "to bring to an end by action," we have not got very far. If we say that both pertain to "change" or "motion," we have only moved from the cryptic to the more cryptic.

The Latin noun *actus* derives from the verb *ago*, its Greek brother being 'ÁGO. The latter is close to PHÉRO, which we encountered in "metaphor." And 'ÁGO meant originally to lead or drive cattle. All beginnings are simple and clear! AGO was used with cattle or persons, PHÉRO, with things. The phrase, 'ÁGEIN KAÌ (and) PHÉREIN, means to carry off the spoil of the land, both cattle and moveables. From this simple beginning came later meanings of lead, guide, and still more metaphorical ones like "to take a wife."

Ago even in an abridged Latin dictionary takes more than a three-column page, but its original meanings are those of 'ÁGO. *Ferre et agere*, like its Greek equivalent, meant to carry and drive off, that is, to rob and plunder, the commonest way in the past to win fame and fortune and wives. Many of the later meanings of *ago* pertained to doings in law courts. An *actor*, besides being a driver, was one who took legal action, that is, a plaintiff. It also meant what is its chief meaning for us, a player. This meaning so completely dominates our "actor" that we cannot call anyone an actor without implying that he is a player, a feigner. The noun and verb "act" are not so limited.

An *agitator,* so little like his present-day descendent, was a driver of cattle and later a driver of a chariot in the Roman circus. *Agito,* though coming from *ago* and also meaning to drive cattle, developed excitable overtones of driving violently, to hunt, chase, and pursue wild game, and to rouse, force, or impel. *Actus* (for *ag-tus*) meant the right of driving cattle through a place, then any piece of public business, and, more generally, any doing or performing.

Close to *ago* and *agito* is *pello,* which means to drive, thrust, to turn away, to drive into banishment, to rout the enemy, and so on. *Pello* compounded with several prepositions gives us "compel," "impel," "propel," "repel," and "dispel." "Compel" and "impel" mean to force or constrain another to do something. And "force," we know is *fortis,* valor or courage, the virtue or power of a man (*vir*); and both "strain" and "constrain" are from *stringo,* to draw tight. To compel something, an act of "compulsion," requires that we strain our muscles and tendons and, metaphorically, our nerves.

If spirit is an alien in this world of matter, a transcendent being that has inserted itself within the interstices of our gravid flesh, as some maintain, then, as a consequence of its fall into matter, it has lost all vestiges of its former being and must form its images and ideas entirely from the stuff of this world. Just as "spirit" is a sign, written, spoken, or whispered to one's self, to designate the activity of linking signs called symbolizing, so "acts of the spirit" are metaphors made from

64

cattle driving, beating the bush for game, straining muscles and sinews in contests with adversaries, and displaying those powers that a tense, alert, and forceful man displays.

As we know, muscles are tense because they are stretched (which is only saying "muscles are stretched because they are stretched"). But what is "attention?" Why, of course, *ad-tendo,* to stretch out towards something. To restate a famous dictum of Aristotle, there is nothing in or of the spirit that was not first in or of the body.

By the metamorphosis of metaphor a compulsion is also that which constrains us to obey an "inner" impulsion or impulse. The usual characteristic of an impulse is that it is impulsive, that is, without prevision. In one sense an impulsive act is an act of free-will, for it is spontaneous (*sponte,* of free will), coming freely from the heart and not impelled by external constraint. In this sense an instinct (*instigo,* to goad or prick) is also, to be redundent, a spontaneous act of free will. But in a stricter meaning of the word, an impulse may be free, but it is not spontaneous. Back of the verb *spondeo* is SPÉNDO, to pour out a drink-offering to a god before drinking wine, the Latin-derived name for the act being "libation." With the practical Romans *spondeo* meant to make a solemn promise to fulfill a business or legal agreement. Only a responsible man would make such an accountable response.

An act that bears this mark cannot be either compulsive or impulsive, for it must be *deliberate,* that is the result of balancing one impulse against another (*libra* is the balance of scales and *libro* means to balance). Such an act of weighing one impulse against another and choosing among them is a voluntary act. Goodness knows what reams of nonsense have been written about *"the will."* "Willing" denuded of all reification, is only conscious, deliberate weighing as contrasted to involuntary impulse. *Volo* means to will, wish, desire, propose, and its Greek equivalent is BOÚLOMAI, with similar meanings. *Volentia* meant pleasant and agreeable things, and *volens,* willing, eager, ready.

Pleasant and agreeable things are what all men desire. A desire is a conscious kind of impulsion. *Desidero* means to look eagerly towards a thing, and, hence, to long for, to stretch out towards. Anything that we stretch out towards in this manner becomes a determination. A *terminus* is an end, and as we know, determine and define (*terminus* and *finis*) are synonymous. And so we are determined to get to the thing that we look towards so eagerly just as the engineer is determined to get his train to the terminal. For this reason we have purposes in mind; that is, we set before (*pro* plus *pono,* to place) our mind's eye an image of the thing to be attained.

Our image cannot be a very clear one, for it is enshrouded by the clouds of the future. Every time we form a determination that involves a passage of time and space longer, let us say, than an hour and a mile, we are attempting to define an end that lies beyond our vision. It is a part of the wisdom of mankind to recognize that what is supposed to be the end that all men seek—happiness—is a matter of "happenstance," for the "hap" of "happiness" is Old Norse for good luck. It is unwise, therefore, to try to determine one's happiness. "Happiness" is something that happens to the man of good fortune, that is, the lucky man, for the *fors* of fortune means that which happens to chance and *fortuna* is chance or luck.

At every moment of his life a man is the center of a swarm of impulses and desires, and he must, un-Hamlet like, make decisions (*de* plus *caedo,* to cut) by cutting short deliberation. A man of decision is one who is always cutting the Gordian knot of potentiality.

Our admiration for a man of this type should be tempered by the reflection that the virtue most essential to the man of action is prudence, which is not just caution but foresight. *Prudens* is a contraction from *provid-ens* in which the discerning reader should see *pro-video,* to see forward. It is a rare man of action, quick at deciding, who is also a man of providence. Patience is often more difficult than decision.

"Patience" is being patient, and there is a great difference between being patient and being *a* patient. The former is a virtue, and despite etymology, patience is a difficult kind of action. The paradox in this statement is due to the fact that "patience" and patient," as well as "passive," "passion" and "pathetic," come from *patior,* to bear or suffer, and ultimately from PÁSCHO (infinitive, PATHEÎN) , which means to suffer or be affected or moved by anything.

To be passive is to be acted upon rather than to act. When a man is in a passion, he is like one possessed or owned rather than like one in possession of his faculties. A man in a passion is truly a pathetic case, for he is a passive sufferer of things that are befalling him (*cado,* to fall, *casus,* that which chances to fall or happen) . Our Lord's passion is that which befell Him between the Last Supper and His death.

It is the general view, held both by eminent philosophers like Aristotle and by men of affairs, that it is better to act than to suffer, to effect than to be affected, to do rather than to be done to. The example of Christ may be a passive voice on this question, but we shall not heed it for the present.

By the genius of the Greek language and Aristotle its most potent interpreter, all acts are divided into two kinds. There is potential act and act in act. "Potential" derives from *potens,* which is the Latin equivalent of DÝNAMIS, and means able, potent, and *potentia* is ability power, faculty. *Facultas* is from *facilis,* and the latter is from *facio,* to make. Anything easy to make is *facilis.* A college faculty has the ability to matriculate candidates and graduate them (*gradus,* step, grade) step by step until they receive a degree or are degraded. A faculty of the mind is one kind of ability or function, for example, wishing, deciding, perceiving, and so on. "Will power" has nothing to do with "mental force or energy;" all it means is the faculty or capability of willing.

There is an Ancient and a Modern view regarding the kind of activity thinking is. If we follow Aristotle and St. Thomas, thinking is more active and less potential than muscular or physical acts. According to them there is a hierarchy of acts that leads step by step from the inanimate to the animate (*anima,* that which blows or breathes), to the thinking animal, man, and to "the eternally perfect animal," God.

Now the highest kind, the most active and deliberate kind, of thinking is thinking about the highest things or perfect things or last things. These are synonyms, for perfect things are things that have been brought to completion (*per-facio*). Thinking of this kind requires first of all recollection, the collection of our faculties; then meditation, from *meditor,* which may be compared with MÉDOMAI to give heed or attend; and then contemplation, a word of odd derivation.

Contemplate comes from *contemplor,* which means to consider and give attention to, but its original meaning is both more earthly and more unearthly. It meant to mark out a *templum,* or a place for observation on every side. A *templum* (akin to TÉMNO, to cut) is a place or portion cut off by an auger or diviner with his staff where he may observe the auspices. From hence comes our "temple," a place of worship.

Through recollection, meditation, and contemplation we may gain fresh insights or intuitions into ourselves, the world, and our relations to it, and may even in a rare favorable, auspicious moment, as we pant with longing for the ultimate— (last things) , behold the Universe—the One—under the aspect of eternity, a vision which has been the ultimate goal of sages and mystics.

This ancient view of contemplation as the highest act of which man is capable, the perfection of his manhood, is rejected by the Moderns, as a product of the thinking of a small exclusive leisure class in a slave "society." It belongs with the foot-long fingernails of the Mandarin.

The modern view is that thinking is delayed contemplated action, and a scheme (SCHÊMA) that cannot be successfully acted out in the laboratory, the market place, or the assembly is only a wind-egg. The test of an idea or desire is performance, and the measure of a man is not what he knows but what he can do.

Let thy prayers be good deeds. Pragmatist, instrumentalist, and existentialist would say, "Amen!"

CHAPTER 13

ALL GOOD ACTS

A witticism of a certain philosopher is to declare, "All men desire the good;" and then, to the inevitable question, "What is the good?" to reply, "No good." Another reply less cynical but not much more satisfactory is, "The good is what every man desires."

"Good" and "gather" have the same Teutonic root, and the "good" is that which is culled out and collected. The "good" is also that which is fitting and suitable. The comparative and superlative forms will help us to get the proper feeling for the word. This apple is "good," this one is "better," and this one is "best" of the three. The glibness that is a consequence of familiarity often leads us to reify "*the* good" or "goodness," as in the phrase, "The true, the beautiful, and the good." But logically and etymologically we should reify (if we *must* reify) "*the* Best."

As "truth" is a name or label for all speaking and writing that conforms to things and acts, so "good" is a name or label for all those things and acts that we approve of and would either gather to us or imitate if we could.

The good man is said to be the moral or ethical or virtuous man, and having defined the "good" by these assumedly equivalent terms, we think we have said something. Let us see.

All ethical and moral things are acts. We speak of "immoral thoughts," but, strictly speaking, this is rather meaningless. Even a moral or good man in coming to a decision must entertain both good and bad thoughts and, hence, have, "immoral thoughts."

"Ethics" and "ethical" come from 'ÉTHOS, meaning custom, usage, manners, habit. The verb 'ÉTHO means to be accustomed to, to be in the habit; and 'ÊTHOS means both an accustomed place or haunt and custom, usage, habit. In the plural it means disposition, temper, or character.

When Cicero wanted to translate the adjectival form 'ETHIKÓS into Latin, he hit upon *moralis,* which is derived from *mos, moris,* and, plural, *mores,* which is derived from the verb *meo,* the going or the pursuing of one's way, a meaning quite close to 'ÉTHO. Hence *mos* is the will or self-will of a person and so his humor or caprice and, by a surprising twist, usage, practice, custom, habit.

The adjective *morosus* means, in a good sense, resolute attention, scrupulous, and particular; in a bad sense, self-willed, passionate, capricious, perverse, or sour. Etymologically a moral man is a morose man in one or more of its senses, a fact that will not be challenged by anyone who knows a blue-nosed puritan.

It is one of the caprices of speech that a word which originally meant self-willed, capricious action came to mean the exact opposite—namely, habitual, customary action. A habit is a *habitus* (*habeo,* hold, take hold of), the having or holding of one's self in a certain condition. Hence the expression, "a riding habit," a certain mode of dress. Ethical behavior is a doing that is customary with the individual or the group. "Custom" comes from *consueo,* and *sueo* has the same meaning as 'ÉTHO, to be accustomed, to be wont to do. Just as we can mean by "habit" a customary way of acting or a form of dress, so we can speak of a custom or, by a caprice of spelling, a costume.

In short, ethical or moral acts are either the customary, habitual acts of the individual or of the group, but in the developed meaning of the word a moral or ethical act of the individual is one that conforms to the ways of his group. In recent years anthropologists have used the plural of *mos, mores,* to mean folk-ways.

Strictly speaking, anyone who acts unconventionally, so that you cannot depend upon him to do the habitual, proper, expected thing, is not a moral or ethical person. To be conventional is to belong to the gathering, the group, the assemblage *(con + venio,* to come; hence, to come together). To be moved by forces or virtues outside the convention is to be, obviously, an "outsider." Whether the moving force is a divine or diabolical virtue can be known and judged only by the fruits thereof, and these may come to fruition only after the sower has died, not infrequently, a martyr's death.

Anyone so unconventionally motivated must be either an idiot, a madman, a witch, a painted lady, a blue stocking, a bloomer girl, a long-hair, a bohemian, an intellectual, a radical, an outlaw, a genius, or a prophet. Most of these speak for themselves, only three, idiot, genius, and radical, needing to be etymologized here. The "prophet" will be examined later.

"Idiot" derives from 'ÍDIOS, one's own, personal, private, strange, peculiar. "Genius," the Latin *genius,* which derives from the verb *geno,* to generate or beget, originally meant a guardian spirit, like "good angel," but it also signified the unaccountable, outside motivation of an un-accountable person. One may have an evil genius as well as a good genius. It might even be said that a genius is a solitary idiot who universalizes himself!

All radicals, of course, are immoral, for they will not conform and accept the established rules and modes and the generally accepted explanations for them, but insist upon getting down to the root (*radix*) of things and, as a consequence, turning everything topsy-turvy. Though neither they nor their enemies will admit it, the outside force that moves them is the ideal.

Radical educators are always being accused of "indoctrination." No doubt some of them do, but the real educator does not; and yet he is detested just as much as those who do. In fact, the critics of the schools (in current history the attack is aimed at "progressive educators") far from objecting to "indoctrination" want it and nothing else. Consequently, they also want the teachers to be "doctors" and not "educators."

A doctor is a *doctor*, that is, a teacher or instructor, because he informs, demonstrates, shows, *doceo*. A doctor will indoctrinate, which is to say that he will teach doctrine, the habit produced by indoctrination. An "educator" in one sense of the verb *educo*, to train or rear, differs little from the teacher of doctrine. Both should be called "pedagogues." The PAID-AGOGÓS (PAîS, child; 'ÁGO, to lead) was the slave who led a child to and from the school and, later, a teacher of children. In another sense of *educo*, to lead out or to lead forth, the teacher will be the kind of teacher that Socrates aspired to be—mid-wife to his students' ideas.

The Greek word for opinion, DÓXA, which also gives us "doxology," gives us "orthodox" ('ORTHÓS, straight, right, true; compare "orthopedics") and "heterodox" ('ÉTEROS, other). The teacher of doctrine inculcates orthodoxy; the educator will necessarily encourage some kind of heterodoxy.

Customary ethical and moral acts are of two kinds: unwritten and written or codified (a *codex* was a board spread with wax for inscribing). The former are called "customs" and the latter, "laws." It is usually assumed that laws are more binding or obligatory than customs, but the reverse is generally the case. Customs, like keeping up with the Joneses, may drive those who break them to suicide, whereas laws are evaded with impunity by both outlaws and those wealthy enough to employ clever lawyers. Sometimes a law is so contrary to first and second nature that nearly everyone breaks it.

The upright man is one who respects "the right" and is justly praised for his rectitude (*rectus,* right, straight). He has no use for innovations in government, and once a bill, a proposition reduced to writing, receives the sanction (*sanctio,* from *sancio,* to make sacred or inviolable) of a number of rightly appointed or elected representatives, he calls it a law, something laid, fixed, or established, and tries to conform to it. For if it is a good law, it simply states in writing something that conforms to custom. He will even conform to bad laws, knowing that they run counter to the ethical or customary sentiments of the group and will be eventually repealed or become just dead statutes (*statuo,* to stand, place, establish).

It is the code of the upright man to follow the established mode, for a *modus* (*metior,* to measure) is a measure. Also for this reason he admires modesty (*modestus*). Even his gait is a measured one, and in all of his acts he is guided by rule (*regula,* a straight stick, a guide, a ruler). His friends call him a righteous man; his enemies, a self-righteous man. Though he may not be dexterous (*dexter,* right *dextera,* the right hand) he can always offer the right hand of fellowship, for he belongs to the right groups and he is always opened-handed except to those about whom there is something sinister (*sinister,* left; *sinistra,* the left hand), especially those of the political left.

As important as "right" is in all that pertains to him, there is another sign just as important. This is "stand." The most obvious examples are "standing" and "standards," which he highly values. Others less obvious but just as important enter into the fabric of his thinking about governing and being governed.

A sound constitution (*con* + *sto,* stand), whether applied to a man or a body of laws, is one that can stand the test of crises (κρίσις, a separating, a putting apart, a deciding, a choosing). A wise legislator (*lex, legis,* law) is one who institutes (*in* + *statuo,* to cause to stand, put, place) sound institutes, that, is laws. And the soundness of both an institute and a constitution is established in terms of stability.

The institutions of a state (*status,* from *sto,* stand), if they are to stand, should consist of customs, traditions (*trado,* to give up, hand over, transmit), and laws that express the will of the people.

Justice depends upon a people being bound and united together (*jus, juris,* is that which morally joins or unites

75

together). Evidence of this kind of union is uncoerced loyalty, that is, keeping faith with the law (Old French *loial* from *legalis*). The greater the awareness of a people that there are two kinds of law, one for the poor and one for the rich, the greater will be their awareness of injustice and the justification for their disloyalty.

Are all good, ethical, moral, upright, upstanding, just men virtuous? Within one quite modern meaning of the word, yes; otherwise, not necessarily.

Virtus is the quality of the *vir;* and the *vir* (related to Sanscrit *vira,* heroes) is a male person, a man. So a very good translation of *virtus* is "manliness." In Homer all free men, as opposed to slaves, were heroes ('ÉROS). A strong, stalwart, courageous, forcible, upstanding man, one of heroic measure and stature, has virtue.

A good man in the conventional sense may be just a goody-goody without genuine virtue. On the other hand, a scoundrel and murderer like Celleni rightly prided himself on his *virtu,* as indeed he had it in superabundance—physical, intellectual, and artistic virtue. Virtue is, broadly, excellence, and it may be of any kind, including the "virtue" of a drug. The Greek equivalent of "virtue" is 'ARETÉ, and Aristotle distinguished between 'ARETÈ 'ETHIKÉ (virtus moralis) and 'ARETÈ DIANOETIKÉ (intellectual virtue).

A virtuous man is a valiant man, one who is valued. Philosophers are currently concerned over whether or not there is such a thing as value, while the rest of us go right ahead valuing this and putting no value on that.

Valere means to be strong, stout, vigorous, healthy, hale, and hearty. The imperative *vale* is the salutation,

"Be in good health." Thus the verb means to have strength, force, power, influence—in short, to have worth. And what is "worth?" "Worth" is from Old English WEORTH and meant pecuniary value or price. "Give me halfpenny worth of beans" and "He isn't worth a hill of beans" will do better than further definition. "A pearl of great price," "a pearl of great worth," and "a pearl of great value" all mean the same thing. However, for fear of sounding too mercenary, we should add that a worthy man sets no price on his friendly services.

A free man values most of all the priceless pearl of liberty, that is, doing as he pleases. His *libido,* which psychoanalysis has made an English word, is his desire. *Libido,* like *liber,* is akin to *libeo,* to be desired or desirable. It is honorable to be a liberal giver or a liberal in politics, but it is not so commendable to be a libertine, for then one's *libido* becomes a passion and puts one into bondage to his emotions.

Just as all men desire the good, so do all men desire liberty—freedom of action to achieve the goods they are pleased to seek. The problem that history sets before men of a given period is the best way to achieve the liberty, the freedom, to get and secure what they desire —health, wealth, and happiness. Sometimes this is best achieved by centralizing government, as was true in England as a consequence of the Baron Wars; sometimes by decentralizing government, as was true in England with the rise of the middle class in the late seventeenth and eighteenth centuries.

The true liberal is the one who can read the signs of his time and knows which one of these two policies is better suited at *that* time to increase the people's liberties.

CHAPTER 14

BEAUTIFUL THINGS

The good artist and craftsman is supposed to be devoted to Beauty. "Beauty" derives from *bellus,* which comes from *benus,* which equals *bonus,* which, as everyone who has ever received a bonus should know, is the Latin for "good." So beauty is a good, as the French may feel more vividly than we English and Americans, because *bellus* became their *beau, bel, belle* and *bonus* became their *bon.* But even an English or an American belle should be able to see that her beau is both a bonus and a beauty.

The frivolous note is not due to any prejudice against beauty. The relevant words have themselves introduced this irreverent tone. Though a Shelley may indite a hymn to intellectual beauty and a Millay assure us that Euclid alone has looked on beauty bare (like a skeleton?), beauty is inseparably associated in our minds with "pretty" things, with decoration, adornment, and ornament—three Latin-derived words that mean em*bell*ishment, something added to things to heighten sensuous pleasure like paint and plaster to make a pretty face prettier.

This is not said to belittle the kind of aesthetic ('AISTHÉSIS, sensation) enjoyment that embellishment gives, whether it be the enhancement of food by spices and sauces, of a building by fretwork, or a face by salves and pigments. The inseparable relation between love and fine plumage is attested by nearly every living creature from the red comb and irridescent tail of the cock to the finery of beaus and belles at a ball. An inevitable consequence of being in love or seeking to be beloved is to try to win the admiring glance by adornment.

After love as a motive comes the desire to impress one's contemporaries by elegance. The elegant are the elect—at least in good Latin. *Electus* is a participle of and *elegans* an adjective derived from *eligo,* which means to choose, pick out, select *(selego)*.

Renaissance art was so elegant because so many powerful cardinals and princes wanted to demonstrate that they were among the select elect and could be, if they chose, munificent, that is, able to give someone a job *(munificius,* bountiful, from *munus,* post, employment, office, and *facio,* make).

But, seriously, the best way to exorcise this frivolous conception of beauty that we have been entertaining is to take a second look at the most frivolous of all of these words that pertain to beautiful things, namely, "pretty." To say a thing is pretty is almost to damn it—a pretty face, a pretty picture, a pretty ribbon.

"Pretty" is from the Old English *praett,* meaning trick, wile, craft; and "pretty" in Old English meant cunning, crafty, artful, astute; and after the fourteenth century, when applied to a person, meant clever, skillful, apt, and to things, ingenious, artful, clever.

It is too bad that the word lost these meanings and came to mean almost anything that is pleasing in a nice sort of way. We need a word that has this earlier meaning of "pretty"—something done with art, craft, ingenuity, and subtleness in order to weave a spell over the beholder or auditor.

If there were such a term, it would help dispel (no relation to "spell," despite appearances) some of the confusion about art and the aims of the artist. His aim is not "prettyness" nor "beauty." As craftsman his aim is to give his matter a form appropriate to its function. Some early automobiles looked like a surrey with the fringe on top; in recent years as designers have begun to develop a feeling for what they are designing, the true lines of an automobile are beginning to emerge.

The artist, as maker and shaper, is trying to hold up a *new* image of the world—his vision—for us to see. He may want to give us pleasant sensations, he may want to make us laugh, he may even want to shock us into seeing the kind of world we have let come into being, or he may want to communicate the stupendous mystery of being alive.

When we stand before the cage of a tiger, study the curves, color, and texture of a rose; look into the eyes of an old woman; witness an act of courage; or watch the incredible act of birth—what is it we sense? Whatever this is—a momentary awareness of the soul of things, something somehow more important than truth or goodness—this is what the great artist would like us to sense.

We shall have to call it "the beautiful" for the want of a less debased symbol to signify this kind of awareness of our world. The word "sublime" from *sublimis,* uplifted or exalted, was introduced into English to designate the beauty that inspires awe, reverence, and similar lofty attitudes, but it has never really caught on.

The greatest error among patrons of the "fine" arts is to think that artists must mimic reality like a placid pool of water. The musical composer has not had to contend with such nonsense; no one has ever criticized

Beethoven's *Pastoral Symphony* because it did not consist of accurate imitations of twittering birds, mooing cows, neighing stallions, rustling leaves, screaming winds, and claps of thunder. But painters, sculptors, and dramatists have been in bondage to this false notion of their function.

Part of this false notion was due to uncreative medieval and renaissance critics reverently misinterpreting Aristotle's famous observation that "art imitates (*imitor*) or mimics (MIMÉOMAI) nature," not seeing the significance of another common analogy of his that nature is like the artist. Aristotle by such observations was expressing no theory of "copy-catting" but the general and true observation that art brings forth, creates as nature does.

This becomes even clearer when the Latin and Greek words for art are compared. *Ars* derives from *apto,* which means to join. "Art" is skill in joining and fitting. *Ars* came to mean skill in anything from cabinet-making to a learned profession, and the various skills became divided into the liberal and the illiberal arts.

The Greek word for art—TECHNÉ—is from TÍKTO, which means to bring into the world, to bear young, to produce. A participle of this verb, TEKÓN, means father and a TÉKNON is that which is born, a child.

The TECHNÉ and PHÝSIS (nature) of Aristotle had a common denominator of meaning, namely, organic creation and birth, that is not to be found in *ars.*

Another reason why this false theory of the artist as a copycatter of nature persisted in stultifying the visual arts was the need for copyists to make accurate portraits and illustrations for books. Now at last the camera, an art product, has liberated the painter to use his materials creatively (technically) .

CHAPTER 15

THE MANY AND THE FEW

Though mankind is *one* race, men persist in making various artificial distinctions and classes, one of the most recent being "the haves" and "the have-nots." This is a more honest division than some, for it does backhandedly pay lip-service to the ideal of social equality expressed in a document like *The Declaration of Independence*. Other such distinctions have been less flattering to the multitude.

"Multitude" is the central idea for many of these unflattering distinctions. On the one hand there is quantity and on the other "the quality," as the eighteenth century termed the select few.

"The voice of the people," which today falls rather pleasantly on our democratic ears, seems less impressive as "the voice of the many," which is the original Latin meaning of *populus,* seen a little more clearly in the Greek adjective for many, POLÚS. The Greek 'OI POLLOÍ, the many, was popularized in America by that enemy of the people, Henry L. Mencken, along with one of his tasteless coinages, "the booboisie."

The more literary term "plebeian" means about the same thing as the "populace," only the Latin original had for the Romans a slightly lower connotation. *Plebs* is related again to a Greek word that better divulges its central idea, PLÊTHOS, a great number, a mass, a plethora. Tò PLÊTHOS was the people, the commons, the masses.

"Mob" is another dyslogistic term for the many. It is a shortened form of *mobile,* which is short for *mobile vulgus,* the excitable crowd. An Englishman in 1679 wrote, "Ye mobele was very rud to Ye Dutch Imbasidor." Erratic movement is one characteristic of the multitude; another is that the "mobile" will crowd and press upon each other and, worse, upon any member of the quality unfortunate enough to be caught in the throng. Hence "the crowd" and "the press." The former is still with us; the latter has dropped out of usage, and Shakespeare's line seems odd to us:

"Who is it in the presse, that calls on me?"

The crowd is also characterized by low speech, that is, according to the quality—the fops, and the countesses, and the poetasters. Philologists, who acknowledge the multitude, the people, as the true makers of language, disagree with this view, though admitting that many of the words of the folk justify the supercilious eyebrows of highbrows.

The crowd to these fastidious critics are a lot of gabblers. The Dutch equivalent of gabble is *rabbelen,* so . . . the crowd are the rabble. Obviously too, the rabble have no manners or taste, as have the quality. So a Latin word for the rabble, *vulgus* give us both "vulgar" and "vulgate." "Vulgarity" is one of the most insulting things that can be said about a person, but "The Vulgate" means the common, ordinary edition of the Bible.

Should the Scriptures be translated into the vernacular? has been a vulgar issue in the history of Christendom. *Vernaculus,* from *verna,* a home-born slave, means domestic, indigenous, native; and so the vernacular is the speech of natives. Vulgar people speak the vernacular. And the *Vulgate,* the Latin Bible, of the fourth

83

century was not too far from the vernacular. Later opposition of the Roman Church to translation of the Bible into vernacular French, German, and English was an example of inconsistency arrogated to a principle.

Let us turn now to "the quality," the few. The Greek, as usual, gives us the word for it. Over against 'οι πολλοί are 'οι 'ολίγοι, the few. And 'ολίγος + 'άρχω, to rule, give us one form or theory of government, oligarchy.

There are those wise men or cynics who aver that systems may come and go, but there is really only one enduring political system—oligarchy, the rule of a few who belong, strictly, not to the right crowd, but to the right few. Others while giving partial assent to this view maintain that it is not exclusive enough. The few, of course, but which few?—'οι πλοῦτοι, the rich, or 'οι 'άριστοι, the best? In the one case you will have a "cracy" (κρατέο, to be strong and mighty, to rule) by the rich, a plutocracy; in the other, one by the best, an aristocracy.

A further step toward exclusiveness in government is made by those who agree with Homer: "The rule of many is not good; let one be the ruler." However, these advocates of unanimity are not unanimous in their advocacy of monarchy (μόνος one 'άρχω, to rule). Some advocate a king, because a king belongs to the right tribe (*cynn*) or an emperor because he knows how to command or order (*imperare,* to command) ; or a dictator, because he can order and declare (*dicto*) and what he dictates become *dicta;* or, possibly, a Czar or Kaisar like Caesar, whose name by accident or deeper design means "hairy one."

Time's clock being a whirligig, there are today many sound Republicans (*res,* things + *populus, . . .* the mob?) , who weary of democracy ("cracy" by the δῆμος, the mob), sick of socialists (*socius,* a fellow-sharer, comrade, companion) , if not of society (*societas,* fellowship, association, union) , and so fearful of communism (*communis,* serving and sharing together, from *com + unus,* one) that they have become suspicious of "community," "communication," "communion," and "common."

It is much more than a play upon words to say that fear has been the mother of xenophobia (ΧΈΝΟS, stranger, + PHÓBOS, fear) . The strange and different is always more likely to invoke distrust rather than trust, whether it be strange appearances or strange ideas. Outlandish ways and speech—beware! As the Cockney said to his matey, "There's a furriner, Jock. 'Eave a brick at 'im."

"Strange," "extraneous," and "estrange," by different routes derive from *extraneus,* external or foreign, from *extra,* without. Extraneous factors can so estrange a husband and wife that they become strangers to each other.

A foreigner is necessarily a stranger, for the etymological reason that he is someone outside the door (*foris*) ; and surely, men used to think and many, alas, still do, you cannot treat him as a friend, for how can you love (Old English *freond,* a participle of *freon,* to love) a rank outsider?

When men used their plows to plow (*urvo*) the boundary of a city (*urbs*) , that which is marked out by the plow, and left the earth and earthy things for the urbanity of city-dwelling, they gained much and they lost much, as the modern movement back to the suburbs is demonstrating.

However, language offers little support for the view that there is something to be said for the country and country folk as well as for the town and townsmen. For one reason, the city folk first lived in citadels and exploited the country (*contra,* that which lies opposite). Counts, courtiers, courtesans, and other cohorts (*cohors, cors,* an inclosure, a court) who learned to pay court and perform other courtesies have been responsible for depicting rural life (*rus, ruris,* country) as fit only for rustics, boors (akin to German *bauer,* peasant), and clowns (peasants).

Another reason was that the livelihood of grammarians (GRÁMMA, letter) rhetoricians ('RÉTOR, orator), poets, actors, and playwrights depended upon flattering the whims and opinions of these gentry of the court. The boors and clowns who are the laughing-stock and clod-hoppers of Shakespeare's plays, are illiterate peasants (those who belong to the *pays,* the country), who maul the King's English.

French *pays* derives from *pagus,* a country district or canton. So, as you might know, words pertaining to country folk rather than to godless city folk became appelations for those outside the circle of Christendom—"pagan" and "heathen," the latter, of course, coming from "heath-dweller."

The Greek equivalent of *pagus* is DÊMOS. Those who dwell in a deme or township are the common folk, the masses, the mob; and one possible translation of DEMOKRATÍA is "mobocracy."

In contrast to DÊMOS is PÓLIS, the city. The city dwellers are the true insiders whose accents are cultivated and who not only know the latest thing but also that every man has his price, especially if he is a politician. Politics, the management of a PÓLIS and the making of policy and drawing up polities, *is* politics.

For reason that philologists and historians may quarrel over PÓLIS has given us some words with an odor of corruption, whereas *civis,* a dweller, gives us such words as "civic," "civics," "civil," "civility," "civilize," and "civilization;" and a derived form *civitas* gives us, by way of the French, "city" and "citizen."

The slow process of transforming quantity into quality has taken a long and devious time, as language testifies. One evidence is the way that the ranks and titles of one age lose their significance and are replaced by others.

As might be guessed by anyone knowing the nature of patriarchal society, many titles of rank and honor come from words for fathers and graybeards.

A patrician, as opposed to a plebeian, is one, etymologically, who plays a paternal (*pater*) role in the state. He who plays a similar role in the church is called "father" or *padre* or, if *pontifex maximus,* "Pope," from Latin *papa.* Anyone who has paternal feelings about his country is a patriot. A good patriot is opposed to paternalism in government as much as he is to nepotism (*nepos,* grandson or nephew).

The Roman title "Senator" came from the same source as "senile"—namely, *senex,* old. Though all senators are elders, all elders are not senile. The Greek equivalent of *senex* is PRESBÝTES, an old man; and Presbyterians are a sect that is captained by presbyters or elders. "Captained" rather than "governed" was used, because, technically speaking, a captain is a head (*caput*), whereas a governor is one who steers a boat (*guberno* from

KUBERNÁO). We "really" should speak of the governor of a ship and the captain of a state.

All the various kinds of sirs—sir, sire, *monsieur,* monsignor—are all senators, that is, old men for they derive from *senior,* older or elder. *Monsieur* is "my senior."

In England in the eleventh century a new social class came into prominence, Gentlemen, whose right it was to bear arms, though not a member of the nobility. "Gentle" originally meant anything but "gentle." It comes from *gentilis,* of the same *gens* or race. A *gentilis* was a person who belonged to the same clan or house. A "gentleman" is, literally, a "clansman." Common people and levelers did not care for gentlemen, as the old couplet reveals:

> When Adam delved and Eve span
> Who then was the gentleman?

The upshot of such potshots at one branch of the lesser nobility is that today everybody is a gentleman unless he behaves in a really vulgar manner.

Everyone today is also a "Mister," which is a weakened form of "master," which calls attention to the odd fact that while an adult man has the title "Mister," his young son will on formal occasions have the title, "Master." Some masterful mister wrote in 1674, "I refused a Mr. of arts."

The degradation of the title becomes clear as soon as we discover that "master" comes from *magister,* he that is great. A *magister populi* was a chief of the people, that is, a dictator. Etymologically, all masters or misters should be magnanimous magnates, which being translated is "great-minded great ones" (*magnus,* great + *animus,* mind, and *magnus*).

Chapter 16

FIRST AND LAST THINGS

All beginnings are hard, but so are all endings. Many thinkers before and after Hegel have perceived both of these truths and also the truth that one implies the other. Poe is only one writer who began at the end in the writing of his stories and then moved back to a good beginning for his ending. "The last," we are told in another connection, "shall be first, and the first last."

The future is fortunately hidden from us, but if we could see clearly, we would see that not only do beginnings determine ends but ends determine beginnings. We are not being speciously paradoxical, or cryptic, or mystical, but merely pointing to the profound truth that the beginning, the middle, and the end of a well-wrought play, the life of a man, of a nation, or of mankind constitute one whole.

If we saw with the eyes of a seer, we could read the outcome of a life. Breeders can do this a little. Out of a litter of pups or a group of foals they can read correctly the promise in this pup or this foal, whereas the uninitiated sees only an awkward ungainly creature no different from others. Some perceiving teachers have this insight into children and can see the promise years before the fulfillment. This is not undemocratic doctrine. Abraham Lincoln *was* Abraham Lincoln when he was ten years old and would walk ten miles for a book as he was when he was fifty-four and wrote and re-wrote the Gettysburg Address, and a few discerning people dimly saw in the boy of ten the promise of the man of fifty-four. Though the lines of a man's palm can tell us nothing about his future, his very gestures can if we are that rare person, a truly sensitive contemplator of the signs and one who has learned to read them.

In order to read the signs it is necessary to discover the underlying principle. "Prince," "principal," and "principle" are all related in English as they are in Latin from which they derive. *Princeps* is compounded of *primus,* first, and *capio,* to seize or capture, and so literally it means taking the first place. So in origin and basic meaning there is no difference between a prince and a principal. A principle, with a different spelling, which indicates a different intermediate change from its source *princeps,* is a source of origin and, therefore, an ultimate base or cause, the roots of a thing.

In principio erat Verbum—in the beginning was the Word—begins the Latin version of the Gospel of John, and in the original Greek it is 'EN 'ARCHÊ 'ÊN 'O LÓGOS. And 'ARCHÊ like *principio* means first or beginning, which explains "archaeology," and chief, which explains "architect." It also means a first principle.

One who seeks first principles is a true radical. All radical movements in art, politics, religion, and philosophy always involve an attempt to go back to first beginnings in the very process of making innovations. This is a profound paradox, which, if properly understood, leads to the uncovering of many hidden treasures. This dual movement in time may be seen in modern times in the Romantic Movement, Pre-Raphaelite painting, contemporary art (the influence of primitive art on painters like Picasso), the Christian sects like the Quakers who "return" to primitive Christianity, the periodic returns to Plato, Aristotle, St. Thomas, or even the Pre-Socratics, the importance of studies on primitive communism to Marxists, and so on. There is scarcely any revival of learning or innovation in technique that has not involved such a "backward" reconnaissance. Nor are the sciences, including mathematics, exempt from this principle. The innovators always go back to move forward; their imitators and followers also go back . . . and stay there. A sound principle not only looks back to beginnings; it looks forward to ends.

We speak of cause and effect. What do we mean? Since the origin of the Latin *causa* is obscure, we must depend upon a later and more sophisticated definition— reason or motive. The verb *causor* means to give a reason for something. The greek word 'ΑΙΤΙΑ conveys a simpler meaning—origin, ground, or blame. The verb derived from it means to place the blame, to answer the question in a court of law, "Who is to blame?" What is to blame when a tree dies, an eclipse of the sun occurs, or a man falls down dead. To place the blame is to assign a cause. Aetiology is the branch of medical science that deals with the cause of disease.

An "effect," from the verb *efficio* (*ex* + *facio*, make), is as a noun something caused or produced, but, somewhat confusingly, "effect" as a verb means to bring about, accomplish. "Efficient" comes from the same source; and an "efficient cause," one of Aristotle's four causes, is the only cause that interests modern scientists. They are inclined to scoff at "final causes" dealt with by teleologists interested in proving that the ends (ΤΕΛΟΣ) towards which things move cannot be ignored in getting at the causes of things. The scientists want to know how the end of something can be in any sense a cause.

91

We are trying to intimate that perhaps in the interest of simplicity and efficiency they have concentrated upon the "pushes from behind" and ignored the "pulls from up in front." The movement of anything in time and space from position A to position B is as much due to circumstances and substances at position B as they are to those at position A.

The elusive little word "why," Old English *hwi,* which is the instrumental case of "what" (*hwaet*) has many elusive meanings, and some contemporary scientists cut through the thicket of obscurity by roundly declaring that they do not attempt to answer the question "why?" but only "how?" Only children want to know the "why of things."

Children, then, are wiser than the scientists. It is an intricate problem of etymology, but "why," and "what," and "how" are all derived from "who."

Is it possible that scientists are loathe to attempt answers to the "why of things" because they are even more loathe to attempt an answer to the "who of things?" Not that we are blaming them for this. It constitutes that mode called modesty and deserves commendation.

There is a group of persons, however, who do not follow this mode of behavior and yet admire and try to conform to a mode quite similar to it, only more so, called "humility," which literally means "being dirt!" It comes from an adjective derived from the noun *humus,* meaning the ground, the soil. These people of the lowly dirt make exorbitant claims: they know both the "why and the who of things." They know, or claim to know, first and last things and declare that time shall be no more. Some are called prophets and others priests.

CHAPTER 17

GOD'S VOICES

Though scientists look askance at final causes or the end towards which all mankind moves, there are others who would read the shadows cast by past events and tell us the shape of things to come. These are the men who say forth or foretell. The Greek for "foretell" is PRÓ-PHEMI, and hence "prophet;" the Latin is *praedico*, and hence "preacher." A preacher who announces glad tidings is an evangelist. 'EUAGGELISTÉS is a messenger of good tidings, for 'EU means well or good, and 'AGGÉLLO means to bring tidings or news. Since an 'ÁGGELOS is an angel or messenger, it is not far-fetched to define an evangelist as an angel of good news, or an angel of the gospel, for the gospel is the *gōd-spell*, the good tale.

Prophet, preacher, evangelist. We need one more *persona* to complete the cast of our mystery play—the priest. We have met him before, for he derives from the Greek word for elder, which is the comparative, PRESBÝTEROS of PRÉSBYS, an old man. A priest or a presbyter is an "older old man" or "elder." And though this is so, Presbyterians would strongly object to their elders being called priests, and Roman Catholics would equally dislike having their "fathers" called elders.

If we could trust such signatures of the *Logos*, this one would help explain why prophets are always at loggerheads with priests: the latter being old men are rather set in their ways and dislike news from another quarter.

Whatever the explanation, it is a fact that the history of religion is largely a record of the quarrel between prophet and priest. The former, offering a new vision of things to come, usually denounces the priest for being a pharisaical formalist, ritualist, and hypocrite. The latter, faithful to a previous revelation, strives to silence the former by excommunication, deportation, stoning, crucifixion, hanging, or burning.

Prophets have a genius for seeing obscure signs and reading in them a significance that the ordinary man misses and that the scientist dismisses as the unrelated effects of unrelated efficient causes. If you cannot measure an event in terms of ergs or some other unit and reduce it to a mathematical formula or equation, it can have significance only for the superstitious.

For the superstitious! Unwittingly the scientific "enthusiast" has brought us into the presence of a mystery. "Superstition" is one of those important "stance" words that give us our feeling for the real and sound. These include substance, circumstance, institution, constitution, substitution, transubstantiation, and establish—words composed of various prepositions with variations on *sto,* to stand; statute, statement, and state from *sto;* and native English words like stand, stance, standing, standards, and understand. By means of our understanding, we must get beneath these odd and yet so important terms.

As we have seen, we understand a thing, whereas the Greeks "over-stand" a thing ('ΕΠΊΣΤΑΜΑΙ). But "superstition" comes from *superstitio,* compounded of *super* and *sto,* and literally means to "over-stand" or "above-stand," which is remarkably like the Greek "understand." Just why "understand" is the word for one of the noblest

94

functions of the mind and "over-stand" for one of the most severly criticized mental outlooks is one of those mysteries of language for which there is no satisfactory explanation. It just happened that way.

The linguistic kinship of "understand" and "superstition" should make us a little more charitable towards the latter. There is also another reason. Aside from its grosser expression in irrational fear and awe of the unknown, superstition is substantially nothing more than a vague and confused intimation of the principle that understanding attempts to substantiate—namely, that every substance, without exception, is intimately, inextricably related and united with every other substance —in short, that the universe is one substance subject to one principle.

The average man, uncivilized primitive or urban modern, knows this intuitively and is not bothered by the need to substantiate it. He knows that there is nothing accidental about either his birth or his death, for his number is up at the time. The scientist scoffs at such an absurd notion and yet spends his life trying to reduce to a scientific statement the truth that the universe is a unity and that nothing happens by happenstance.

Since the prophet has no doubt about this principle that the scientist attempts to demonstrate, everything has significance for him, and he reads the signatures of the divine in the fall of a stone or a sparrow, in the flights of birds, in the vanity of rulers, and the murmurs of the people. Omens (*oro*, to speak) speak and tokens (*taecean*, to teach) teach that the spring or winter of this people is nigh.

When he speaks, he delivers oracles (*oro*), and what he utters is a *fatum* (*for*, to say or speak), one's unavoidable fate or destiny. And once more we stand in the presence of a standing mystery, for *destino* (*de* + *sto*) is to make to stand, to make firm, to bind. Destiny is that which is pre-established.

The prophet, full of intuitive insights, is in moments of inspiration drunk with imagery, and his words can scarcely keep pace with his vision. It is for this reason (aside from the basic reason that he is usually not a man of letters) that he has seldom written down his visions, but communicates them orally to his disciples.

Imagination is one outstanding trait of the prophet, brother as he is to the poet. The other is emotion, at times of inspiration amounting to frenzy and even epilepsy. In ancient Greece the speaker of oracles was a MÁNTIS (whence the name of the insect, the praying mantis), because his powers became actual during a mania (MAÍNOMAI, to rage, rave, to be drunk with wine or divinity). In this sense mania and enthusiasm mean the same thing. The verb 'ENTHOUSIÁZO comes from the compound adjective 'ÉNTHEOS ('EN, in, THÉOS, god).

Both his abnormal imagination and emotion are due to his more than normal sensitivity to impressions. The prophet "feels-thinks"—no other word will do. His response to the world is a total response, not the convenient compartmentized thinking of Mr. Worldly Wiseman and Mr. Hypocrite. Is it surprising then that the world-anguish and sickness is his anguish and sickness and that for his very sanity he must retreat periodically from the world, live the life of a hermit, and once more achieve a centering of his life?

Another reason for these periodic retreats to silence and the wilderness, other than to restore his virtue (that is, power), is to escape from the greedy demands of his followers. As Mahatma Gandhi wrote, "The sorrows of Mahatmas are known only to Mahatmas." Not being able to understand the simple clarity of his message, his followers demand other evidence of his divine mission than the only two genuine types of evidence—the truth of his message and the sanctity of his life. They demand signs, which is like asking God to semaphore to them; and the sign they want is miracles.

A miracle? Let the tongues of men confound all who seek miracles! *Miraculum* comes from *miror,* which is akin to MEIDÁO. The latter means to smile, and this was also the original meaning of the former. *Miror* then came to mean to admire, admire one's self, and then to be vain, and then to be amazed or astonished. Those who seek signs might do well to contemplate these signs: *miror* gave us "mirror" and "mirage" as well as "miracle," something that is a cause for wonder. How can miracles prove that they are not mirages or something done with mirrors?

The Greek for miracle is THAÛMA and for *miror* is THAUMÁZO. A thaumaturgist is also a miracle-worker, but he can be a false prophet or a charlatan (*ciarratano,* seller of papal indulgences). The miracle-seeker is little more than a sensation-seeker, and all true prophets know this. Works of wonder can prove nothing to anyone who is unable to be filled with wonder and amazement every day of his life as he beholds the manifestations of nature and of mankind.

All prophets find it necessary to speak in fables (*fabula* derives from *for,* to speak), myths (MŶTHOS is anything spoken as contrasted to work 'ÉRGON), allegories, and parables. Because of the prophet's "parabolic" way of speaking there soon develops an esoteric (the comparative of 'EIS, 'ES, in, and so "inner") and an exoteric (from the comparative of 'EK, out, and so "outer") interpretation of the master's words.

There follows then the need for silence by those who know the inner teaching. The Greek word that means to be shut or closed, especially the lips and eyes, is MÝO. Consequently, the ancient religions that maintained secrets revealed only to initiates came to be called mysteries, from MYSTÉRION, which derives from MÝO.

The mystery religions of Greece and the Near East gradually gave way to the mystery religion called Christianity. The Greek equivalent of the Hebrew word, **Messiah, the anointed one, was CHRISTÓS. CHRÍO means** to anoint, and PHÁRMAKA CHRISTÁ means salves. Hence Jesus the Messiah, Jesus the Christ, and Jesus the Anointed means, insofar as language permits, exactly the **same thing. Christians are the anointed ones.**

Certain of their dogmas are mysteries, and certain of their rites, called sacraments, are too, for in Christian Latin "sacrament" was the accepted translation of MYSTÉRION. The sacrament of communion is a mystery in both its original and later meanings, as the doctrinal quarrels over transubstantiation prove.

Transubstantiation is one great mystery of the Anointed Ones; another is the mystery of the Trinity. Though the mysteries are mysteries because they involve "difficulties which human reason is incapable of solving," our pursuit of meanings make these mysteries less mysterious than they would be to the uninitiated.

Our earlier quest for the real with our present feeling for stance (*sto*) and the additional hint that "person" is a rather arbitrary term for either Latin-derived "substance" or Greek-derived "hypostasis" should help us understand what the theologians have to say about the Mystery of the three Hypostases in One.

As for the mystery of transubstantiation, the understanding of which so divides the Anointed, we can get some idea of the controversy by keeping in mind the Aristotelian equation of matter and potentiality and form and function and the distinction between the underlying substance and the accidents that impress the senses.

The prophet's message is the spirit or matter (an interesting example of how antonyms can be synonyms) ; the doctrine and rite become the jealous care of the priesthood. It is difficult to determine which a priesthood hates the most: a heretic, one who chooses ('AIRÉO) for himself or a schismatic, one who splits (SCHÍZO; compare schizophrenia) with the parent group and, in modern labor idiom, forms a splinter group. Both are a threat to mankind's salvation, for lacking infallibility (*fallo,* to cause to fall, to stumble; to deceive, trick, dupe) , they can cause many to stumble into error and damnation.

The prophet can little stomach all these formalistic niceties of the priesthood, and his advent in the world is always accompanied by denunciation of some priesthood that has turned religion into some kind of bingo game for making money.

The message of the prophet, despite his use of allegory and parable, is quite simple, and several Greek words reveal this a little more clearly than their Latin equivalents. For one thing, the prophet preaches repentance (*re* + *poena,* indemnification, expiation, punishment, penalty). The Greek equivalent is METÁNOIA composed of MÉTA, after, and NOÍA thought. METANOÉO, the verb, means to have an afterthought or, in its religious significance, to have a change of mind or heart. The second theme of his message, a corollary of this, is that we must turn away from our present life of sin. The Greek word for acting sinfully is 'AMARTÁNO to miss the mark as an archer may and, hence, to be in error.

The third theme is the shape of things to come when the seeds that men and nations have sown are judged by their fruits. Nearly all prophets are in complete agreement on this matter: what a man sows, this shall he reap. The farmer as farmer knows that if he sows wheat, he will harvest wheat, and if he sows turnips, he will reap turnips. Men persuade themselves that the principle does not apply to their own lives, but they are only missing the mark. What a man aims to be, this he will be in time. Our choices are the seeds that we sow, and their fruition in the future is as assured as the return of the sun in the morning. Try as we will, we cannot get figs from thistles.

This faith in the moral equivalent of the scientist's principle of cause and effect causes the prophet to look with confidence to the future and predict with assurance the unavoidable consequences of error and sin. The day of judgment is at hand! Many religions, with Christianity a good example, are, therefore, concerned with eschatology ('ÉSCHATOS, the superlative of 'EK, out, and so "outermost" or "uttermost"), the study of doctrines regarding final things like death and judgment.

On the day of judgment the elect and the damned will be separated. The elect will be vindicated, for their fruits are the consequences of right choices; the damned will be accursed, for their choices led them to this downward path. The just man is justified, and the unjust man is condemned. Even God could not set aside this principle without doing violence to his own essence. He is a God of wrath and vengeance simply because his law condemns them who have already passed judgment upon themselves.

One great inconsistency in the prophet's message, which priests and dogmatic theologians try in vain to reconcile, is man's freedom to choose freely, to make free decisions, in the face of God's omnipotence and omniscience. Is it not obvious that the elect and the damned have been elected and damned from the beginning of creation, have been pre-destined, pre-determined, pre-established—in short, fated—to be the persons they are and make the choices they do make, that, to use a modern illustration, dead-end kids will make dead-end choices?

Prophets are seldom bothered by logical consistency. A strange, modern prophet, Frederich Nietzsche said, "Do I contradict myself? Then I contradict myself." And an American seer, Ralph Waldo Emerson, declared that consistency is the bug-bear of little minds. The prophet, however, has faith that such man-perceived inconsistencies, these partial insights, are somehow reconciled in the One which is God.

The priests and theologians who come afterwards have a difficult role assigned to them. They must be apologists and devote time to apologetics ('APÓ, back + LÓGOS, literally, back-speech or talking back) ; otherwise hostile critics would soon make nonsense of the sayings of the prophet or prophets. It must be added that the priests are not "apologetic" in their "apologetics," nor do they tolerate the view that the various accounts of the prophet's life are only so many "apologues," despite the fact that these three words have the same source.

101

Another knot, hard to unravel, is how is it possible to reconcile God's justice and His forgiveness, His wrath and His love? Various religions have their own answers; the Christian answer is the doctrine of Grace. The word is full of obscurity in English because we have lost sight of its primary meaning of favor, kindness, and mercy. "Grace" derives from *gratia,* and *gratia* is the quality of the *gratus,* beloved, dear, favored. The Greek equivalent is CHÁRITOS, the genitive of CHÁRIS, grace, kindness, goodwill. From it we get "charity," a word now so debased it means to most of us giving grudging alms to the indigent.

Rolls and reams and books have been written to expound the doctrine of God's favor, charity, or grace—that is, speaking modern idiom, why God should "play favorites"—without ending the controversy. The two great schools of Christian theologians, Augustinians and Thomists, have each accused the other of being fatalists; and if there is no agreement among them, it would be foolhardy for the rest of us to try to solve the riddle.

The Grace of God is and will remain a mystery, but the grace of man for man is something we should be able to understand, even though after two thousand years of Christianity we still esteem the aggressive, self-sufficient virtues (*vir*) that moved males in a patriarchal cattle-, slave-, and woman-stealing "society" rather than the feminine virtues of gentleness, kindness, service, forgiveness, and sacrifice except on Sunday when the lion of Rome ceremoniously lies down with the Lamb of God (*Agnus Dei*).

The Greek-derived word, "charity," despite its unfortunate fall from grace mentioned above, again gives us a clue to why the glad tidings of Christianity were

102

intended to be a new dispensation *(dispensare,* to weigh out; compare "dispensary"), a new deal for man. The glad tidings of the New Deal were the gospel of love— a love quite different from the pagan worship of Aphrodite, Astarte, Priapus, or Eros (Cupid), to say nothing of Mammon.

And yet though the pagans worshiped at these shrines, they had words for the new kind of love that are strangely lacking in the English lexicon, though it has many different verbs for hate and fear. Our verb, "to love," (like German *lieben*) must serve to express the whole gamut of love from sexual lust, libidinousness, lasciviousness, cupidity, and eroticism to affection, friendship, amity, and "Platonic love."

We have nouns and adjectives for these actions, but from the Latin and Greek sources that we got some of these *(libido, lascivus, cupidus,* 'EROTIKós), we borrowed no verbs. Perhaps, in some respects, this is no cause for regret, but we do need and should have borrowed two Greek verbs— PHILÉO and 'AGAPÁO—and their noun and adjective forms.

From PHILÉO, to love, befriend, in combination with 'ÁNTHROPOS, man; LÓGOS, word; and SOPHÍA, wisdom were formed the important words "philanthropy," "philology," and "philosophy"; and, ironically, the same verb in combination with 'ANÉR, 'ANDRÓS, man, gave us one verb "to philander."

PHILÉO and PHÍLOS, friend, convey the same sense as our noun "friend" (Old English *freond; freon* means, to love); and in "befriend" we almost have the verb we need.

The gap in our *Logos* is all the more reprehensible, for the writers of the New Testament chose deliberately to convey the Christian meaning of love by PHILÉO and 'AGAPÁO. The latter means to be fond of and love dearly in an intellectual rather than a sensual way. The noun 'AGÁPE means brotherly love, charity. The early Christians gathered to break bread together and share things in common, and they called such a love feast, an 'AGÁPE.

In Chapter 21 of the *god-spel* according to St. John, when the resurrected saviour thrice asks Peter whether he loves him or not, Jesus uses the verb 'AGAPÁO in the first two questions, and PHILÉO in the third; and in each of his affirmative replies Peter uses PHILÉO.

St. Paul's great Christian homily on love (I Corinthians, Chapter 13) begins with the stirring declaration:

"Though I speak with the tongues of men and angels, and have not charity ['AGÁPEN] I am become as sounding brass or a tinkling cymbal,"
And ends with:

"And now abideth faith, hope, charity ['AGÁPE], these three, but the greatest of these is charity ['AGÁPE]."

It was this 'AGÁPE, this charity for man, that ushered in the truly human era. Without this love man remains an animal no matter how elegantly he may be groomed and oiled, no matter how cultivated his senses and intellect may be, no matter how much he enjoys good fellowship (*feoh*, cattle, property) and glows with *gemütlichkeit*.

For this Christian love negates normal animal nature, as Nietzsche saw and mocked; this love causes a man to die to the things of the flesh and resurrect to the things of the spirit, both to consider the stars and to have compassion on the fallen sparrow. This love is the true elixir of the alchemists; for it has the power to transmute sensible and intellectual things into spiritual things and to stir both heart and mind to attend to God.

104

CHAPTER 18

ONE

We have been listening to the speech of men in order to try to understand what they have been saying about their living experience. One of the great symbols with which they try to signify the depth and height of this experience is "God." What, who, where, when, why, and how—to use the good reporter's questions—is God?

The word "god" does not help us much to answer these questions. Significantly, perhaps, "god" has no history; it is lost in the darkness of Teutonic barbarism. Those who would derive it from "good" are engaging in etymologizing by appearances, than which there is nothing more misleading.

Philologists hypothesize that "god" is derived from an Old Teutonic *Guđo,* its primary meaning being "what is involved" or "what is worshipped by sacrifice." If we accept this, then "god" tells us nothing about "him" except that "he" is "that which is called upon for favors."

The Hebrew name for God, Jehovah, is really no name at all. It was (and is) in the Hebrew manuscripts a mysterious symbol of four consonants YHWH or JHVH, known as the Tetragrammaton (TETRÁS, the number four, and GRÁMMA, a letter). This four-letter word was unpronounceable. Later Hebrew scholars put in the vowel points of the word for lord, "Adonai," intending for the reader to use this verbal substitute for the ineffable Tetragrammaton. Students of Hebrew at the Revival of Learning assumed that these vowel points were a part of the Tetragrammaton, and so the unutterable written symbol became in Latin spelling "Iehova (h)" and, anglicized, finally "Jehovah." It is now thought that the ineffable name was really "Yawe," with the conjectured meaning, "he that is," "the self-existent," or "the one ever coming into manifestation."

The problem is further complicated. The Hexateuch, the first six books of the Old Testament, is a compilation from, chiefly two different sources, and the authors of one of these two versions did not use the Tetragrammaton but "Elohim," which means "gods." Even in the King James Version of the Bible the careful reader can note that there are *two* accounts of creation in the first two chapters of Genesis. The one derives from the document in which YHWH *is* the Creator, and the other in which Elohim *are* the creators.

The upshot is that YHWH, the term for master or lord, "Adonai," and the polytheistic "Elohim" propose more riddles than answers to our initial questions.

The scholarly name for god, "the deity," proves to be one of several interesting kinsmen of dissimilar mien that owe their being to the Sanscrit word for "sky" and "day," *dyō*. This little word for the heavens and day gave rise to the Sanscrit *diva*, which means "divine," and, as a noun, "god;" to the Greek ᴅîos, godlike, excellent, mighty, divine; to ᴅiós, the genitive form of ᴢᴇús, ruler of the lower air and the cause of rain and storms; and to ᴛʜᴇós, god, which give us "theist," "theodicy," and "theology." The Latin children include *Jupiter,* the genitive being *Jovis* and so "Jove;" *dies,* day; *divus,* divine; and *deus,* the "deity." To the Romans *Jupiter* not only signified the ruler of the heavens but even quite literally the heavens, especially on a rainy day.

106

These children of the day appear in other guises also. There is the Teutonic deity *Tiw* (Thor, the god of war). The genitive *Tiwes* combined with *daeg,* day, gives us "Tuesday." Since *Tiw* is also Jupiter and Zeus (a little more evident in Old High German *Zio* and Icelandic *Cyr*) and ultimately *dyō,* day, "Tuesday" could be translated "the day's day!"

Dies is a day of twenty-four hours, and the adjective form *diurnus* resulted in French *jour,* day; and English "journal" and "diary," both meaning a daily record; "journey," a day's work or travel; and "journeyman," a day-laborer.

The journeying of Portugese to the Far East produced one more child of the day that cannot be ignored. Portugese *deos* in Pidgin English comes out "Joss." So "joss-sticks" are really "god sticks" or, listening to echoes from an earlier day, "day-sticks" or "sky-sticks."

The pattern of evolution of names of the deity is the general pattern, of which we have seen so many cases—from the tangible to the intangible, as the source becomes lost in the mists of the past.

"Hero" ('ÉROS) offers a good illustration of this principle. In Homer "hero" meant all freemen as opposed to bondsmen and slaves; in Hesiod's *Theogony* it meant those warriors who fell before Thebes and Troy; in a still later writer, Pindar, it meant a race of beings between gods and men; and in still later times it meant inferior local deities including legendary founders of cities like Theseus.

The names of the "supreme being" or since "supreme" comes from the Latin superlative *superus,* upper—the "uppermost being" begin their day as the day and as some of its more awe-inspiring celestial manifestations like thunder and lightning and rain storms, and similar voices out of the whirlwind and become translated into almost empty abstractions formed, chiefly, by the superlatives of certain prepositions and adjectives. Whether a catalogue of perfections (*perficio,* to finish, complete), including those magniloquent emblems—omnipotent, omniscient, and omnipresent—point to anything real or nothing at all is a grave matter which each man must weigh in accordance with his own inner light.

It is well to see, however, how easily familiar words heard over and over again, like the monotonous tick of a clock, can cast a hypnotic spell over us. The "supreme being" seems to say so much. But what about the "uppermost being," which expresses the same idea? The "all highest" sounds all right; but if "supreme" and "all highest," why not "most distant," "lowest," and "all deepest?" for surely, the deity is not to be found in just one direction from us—up!

This preference for having the deity "up in the air" (we are not trying to be funny; we *are* trying to stimulate a re-examination of certain fixed ideas and associations) suggests that our "verbal reflexes" differ little from those of ancient Romans, Greeks, and Hindus who looked up in awe at the sky overhead.

The consensus of opinion among theologians is that the deity is somehow both a transcendent (*transcendo,* compounded of *trans,* across, over, beyond + *scando,* to climb, ascend) being exalted above the universe and apart from it and an immanent (*in* + *maneo,* stay, remain, abide) being dwelling, not only in the universe, but within us, nearer than hands and feet.

Such obvious contradictions, paralleled by similar ones in philosophy and logic, raise the question of whether the signs and symbols that have flowered in the soil of human experience are not being pushed to perform functions beyond their powers. How can the finite creature with his all too human signs and symbols speak, except anthropomorphically and fallibly, about God's will, intelligence, love, mind, and other faculties? Why, indeed, do we persist in using the masculine pronouns "He" and "Him" in referring to God instead of the feminine pronouns "She" and "Her" except for the historically accidental custom that this has been a man's world from patriarchal times to the present?

St. Thomas Aquinas, confronted with this impasse, developed the doctrine of analogy or proportion. When we speak of God, we speak neither univocally nor equivocally but analogously—a subtle, difficult, and debatable solution of the problem that we can only allude to here.

An earlier anonymous Christian theologian of the fifth century, known as Dionysius the Areopagite, whom Thomas esteemed and constantly quoted, developed the doctrine of the *via negativa* as the ultimate road to a knowledge of God. Through meditation the intuitive mind pierces the veil of terms and concepts and ratios, comes to know God intuitively, and discovers, in the words of the eighteenth century Anglican clergyman and mystic, William Law, that the human personality is itself an "outbirth" of God.

We have encountered once again, as we have several times before, a fundamental psychological and epistemological dualism from which, it would seem, man cannot escape. On the one hand, he lives in a world of signs, symbols, emblems, labels, ratios, and analogies that somewhat illumine his world for him and enable him to be the animal that creates and the animal that reflects. On the other hand, he lives and experiences the "real" with his muscles, senses, and viscera as do his brothers with other talents, Brother Tiger, Brother Lamb, Brother Fox, and Brother Lark.

The signs in books are like sign posts on the road one is traveling. They can help us along the way, but none is so foolish, we hope, as to take the signs for Rome for Rome itself. It would be well if we always avoided the same kind of error in dealing with other signs. They can stand for and point the way to life, friendship, love, courage, fortitude, kindness, wisdom, death, and God, but to know the Real—for these are names for experiences of the real—it is necessary to go behind, beyond, or through the symbols to the experiences themselves.

To go through the symbol in order to achieve direct communion with the other and thereby overcome duality is usually termed the way of the mystic.

In the depths of our being we are all mystics, and if we are not conscious of the fact at this moment, we shall be before we have died. When we have been shaken to the roots by some tremendous experience, we will know the thing that is beyond words.

To be born is to be a neophyte standing before the door of the Grand Lodge and knocking for admission in order to learn the mysteries. To live is to learn them. The time-honored pledge to silence is an ironic joke. The things we learn about the Real can never be communicated, though they may be shared; and all good poets, philosophers, and theologians know this only too well.

110

WORD INDEX

Note: Greek words are in both English small capitals and Greek characters. Latin words are in italics, as well as a few words of other languages.

able, 58
abstract, 45
abstraho, 45
accidental, 95
accido, 32
accustom, 72
act, 7, 63f.
actio, 7
action, 7, 64
active, 7, 64
actor, 7, 63f., 86
actus, 63f.
adduce, 56
adduco, 46
Adonai, 105
adornment, 78f.
ad-tendo (attendo), 65
aequus, 53f.
affair, 36
'AGAPÁO (ἀγαπάω), 104
'AGÁPE (ἀγάπη), 104
agitator, 64
agito, 64
Agnus Dei, 102
˝AGO (ἄγω), 63, 73
'AGORÁ (ἀγορά), 24
'AGOREÚO (ἀγορεύω), 24, 49
agronomy, 25
AIRÉO (αἱρέω), 99
AISTHESIS (αἴσθησις), 8, 78
AITÍA (αἰτία), 91
allegory, 49f., 53, 97
˝ALLOS (ἄλλος), 49
alms, 102
am, 37
'AMARTÁNO (ἁμαρτάνω), 100
amity, 103
'ANÁ (ἀνά), 52
'ANALOGÍA (ἀναλογία), 52f.
analogy, 52f., 109
anemone, 40
'ANÉR, 'ANDRÓS (ἀνήρ, ἀνδρός), 103
angel, 93
anima, 50, 68
animal, 40, 68
animate, 40, 68
animus, 88
anoint, 98

anomalies, 27
anthropomorphism, 109
antonym, 48
apologetic, 101
apologetics, 101
'APÓLOGOS (ἀπόλογος), 101
apologue, 101
appearance, 28
apprehend, 57
apprehendo, 57
apto, 81
archaeology, 90
'ARCHÉ (ἀρχή), 10, 90
architect, 90
˝ARCHO (ἄρχω), 84
'ARETÉ (ἀρετή), 76
aristocracy, 84
˝ARISTOI, 'OI (ἄριστοι, ὀι), 84
arrange, 24
ars, 81
art, 24, 81
˝ARTHRON (ἄρθρον), 26
arthropoda, 26
artist, 80
'ASTÉR (ἀστήρ), 27
astronomy, 25, 27
atom, 31
˝ATOMOS (ἄτομος), 31
attention, 65
auditor, 13
auger, 69
'AÛS (αῦς), 13
auspices, 69
automatic, 55f.
automaton, 55f.
AUTÓMATOS (αὐτόματος), 55
automobile, 55f.
'AUTÓS (αὐτός), 55
awe, 95

balance, 65
barbarian, 12
BÁRBAROS (βάρβαρος), 12
bauer, 86
be, 32, 39
beau, 78
beautiful, 80
beauty, 78

befriend, 103
beget, 25
beginnings, 89
behavior, ethical, 71
being, 33
belle, 78
bellus, 78
benus, 78
best, 70, 84
blame, 91
blow, 40
blue stocking, 72
bohemian, 72
bomb, 49
BÓMBOS (βόμβος), 49
bon, 78
bonus, 78
boor, 86
BOÚLOMAI (βούλομαι), 66
boundary, 85
bountiful, 79
brain, 16
brave, 6
breath (e), 40
bring forth, 37

cadaver, 43
cado, 42, 67
calculate, 52
calculus, 53
call, 23
can, 58
capio, 90
caprice, 71
captain, 87f.
caput, 87
carnal, 43
carnivora, 43
case, 67
cast, 31
casus, 67
cataloguing, 24
categorizing, 24
category, 26
causa, 91
cause, 91, 94, 100, 102
chance, 32
character, 71
CHÁRIS, CHÁRITOS (χάρις, χάριτος),
  102
charity, 102f.
charlatan, 97
child, 81, 92
choice, 100f.
choose, 99
CHRÍO (χρίω), 98

Christ, 68, 98
Christian, 98, 103f.
CHRISTÓS (χριστός), 98
ciarratano, 97
circumstance, 94
citizen, 87
city, 86f.
civic, 87
civil, 87
civilization, 87
civis, 87
civitas, 87
clan, 25, 88
clarus, 23
class, 22f.
classicism, 54
classicus, 23
classify, 23f., 28
classis, 23
clear, 23
clever, 79
clown, 86
clueo, 23
codex, 74
codified, 74
cognizance, 58
cognoscente, 58
cohors, 86
command, 84
common (s), 9, 29, 82, 85
common sense, 29
commonweal, 36
commonwealth, 9, 36
commune, 9
communication, 85
communico, 9
communion, 85, 98
communis, 9, 85
communism, 85
community, 9, 22, 85
companion, 85
compel, 64
comprehend, 57
com-prehendo, 57
compulsive, 65
compute, 53, 59
com-puto, 59
conceit, 57
conception, 57
concipio, 57
conclude, 60
con-cludo, 60
conjecto, 61
conjecture, 61
connoisseur, 58
consistency, 101

constitution, 75, 94
con-sto, 75
constrain, 64
consueo, 72
contemplate, 69
contemplor, 69
contra, 86
contract, 5
contraho, 5
convello, 5
con-venio, 72
convention, 72
convulse, 5
corps, 43
corpus, 43
cosmos, 28
costume, 72
count, 53, 86
courage, 64
court, 86
courtesan, 86
courtesy, 86
courtier, 86
couth, 58
craft, 79
create, 15
creator, 55f.
creature, 55
crises, 75
crowd, 83
cupidity, 103
cupidus, 103
custom, 71f., 74
cut, 31
cynn, 84

damned, 100f.
datum, 29
day, 107
death, 5
de-caedo, 67
decision, 67
declare, 32
decoration, 78
deductio, 60
deductive, 60
define, 39f., 66
de-finio, 39
degrade, 68
deity, 106
deliberate, 65
deliberation, 67
deme, 86
democracy, 84
DEMOKRÁTIA (δημοκράτια) , 86
DÊMOS (δῆμος) , 84, 86

desidero, 66
design, 21
desire, 66, 77
destino, 96
destiny, 96
determinate, 39
determination, 66
de-termino, 39
deuce, 51
deus, 10, 106
dexter, dextera, 75
dexterous, 75
dialect, 62
dialectic, 62
dialecticize, 11
DIA-LÉGO (δια-λέγω) , 11, 62
diary, 107
dicta (sing., *dictum*) , 84
dictator, 88
dicto, 84
dies, 107
DIÓS (Διός) , 106
disciple, 54
discipulus, 54
disease, 51
disloyalty, 76
dispel, 64
dispensare, 103
dispensary, 103
dispensation, 103
disputation, 62
distribution, 24
diurnus, 107
divine, 106
diviner, 69
divus, 106
do, 29, 63
doceo, 73
doctor, 73
doctrine, 73
door, 85
double-talk, 47
down, 24
DÓXA (δόξα) , 74
doxology, 74
duplicity, 46
dynamic, 7
DYNAMIS (δύναμις) , 7, 69
dynamite, 7
DYS (δυσ-) , 51
dyslogistic, 51

ʾECHO (ἔχω) , 40
economy, 25, 27
educate, 73
education, 73

educators, 73
educo, 73
effect, 91, 100, 102
efficient, 91
efficio (for *ex-facio*), 91
EIDOLON (εἴδωλον), 17
EIDON (εἶδον), 17
EIDOS (εἶδος), 17f., 22
EIMÍ (εἰμί), 32
EIS (εἰς), 98
'EK (ἐκ), 98
elder, 87, 93
elect, the, 79, 100f.
electus, 79
elegans, 79
elegant, 79
eligo, 79
"ELIOS (ἥλιος), 47
elixir, 104
'E LOGIKÉ TÉCHNE (ἡ λογική τέχνη),
    59
Elohim, 106
elucidation, 14
'EMBÁLLO (ἐμβάλλω), 21
embellishment, 78
emblem, 21, 26
"EMBLEMA (ἔμβλημα), 21
emotion, 96
emperor, 84
employment, 6
'EN (ἐν), 40
end, 39f., 89, 91
'ENERGÉO (ἐνεργέω), 7
energetic, 7
engine, 56
entelechy, 40
'ENTHOUSIÁZO (ἐνθουσιάζω), 96
enthusiasm, 96
'EPÍ (ἐπί), 57
'EPÍSTAMAI (ἐπίσταμαι), 94
'EPISTÉME (ἐπιστήμη), 35
epistemology, 3
equal, 54
equate, 53f.
equivocal, 12, 54, 109
equivocate, 54
"ERGON (ἔργον), 6, 55
ergs, 6
"EROS (ἔρως), 103
"EROS (ἥρως), 76, 107
erotic, 103
'EROTIKÓS (ἐρωτικός), 103
error, 100
eschatology, 100
"ESCHATOS (ἔσχατος), 100
esoteric, 98

esse, 38f.
essence, 33, 39
establish, 75, 94
estrange, 85
eternity, 69
"ETEROS (ἔτερος), 74
ethical, 71
ethics, 3, 71
"ETHO (ἔθω), 71f.
"ETHOS (ἔθος), 71
etiology, 91
etymology, 1, 4
EUAGGELISTÉS (εὐάγγελος), 93
evangelist, 93
event, 36
evolution, 25
examination, 24
excommunication, 94
exert, 6
exist, 36
existentia, 36
Existentialism, 37, 69
exoteric, 98
experience, 7
experiment, 7
experior, 7
expiation, 99
exsero, 6
ex-sto, 36
external, 85
extra, 85
extraneous, 85
extraneus, 85

fable, 10, 97
fabula, 10, 97
facere (*facio*), 41
facilis, 68
facio, 79
faculty, 68
faith, 104
fall, 32, 99
fallible, 99
fallo, 99
fantastic, 14
fatalism, 102
fate, 95
father, 81, 87
fatum, 95
fear, 85, 95
feeling, 8
fellowship, 85, 104
feoh, 104
fero, 13, 60
few, 84
figura, 15

figure, 15, 20f., 54
final cause, 91, 93
fingo, 15
finis, 39, 66
finish, 39, 41
flag, 21
folk-ways, 72
follis, 46
fool, 46
for, 10
force, 6, 64
foreigner, 85
foretell, 93
forgiveness, 102
foris, 85
form, 15, 18, 28, 38, 99
forma, 15
formalist, 94
fors, 66
fortis, 6, 64
fortuna, 67
fortune, 67f.
freedom, 77
free-man, 55
free-will, 65, 102
freond, 85, 103
friend, 85, 103
functio, 24
function, 24, 39f., 56, 99
fungor, 39
future, 66, 89

Gaea, 44
GÊ (Γῆ) , 27, 44
gemütlichkeit, 104
general, 25
generalis, 25
generalize, 22, 25f.
generate, 25, 72
genero, 56
genesis, 25
genius, 56, 72f.
GÉNOS (γένος) , 25
gens, 25, 88
gentilis, 88
gentle, 88
gentleman, 88
genus, 22, 25
geometry, 27
gesture, 90
GIGNÓSKO (γιγνώσκω) , 58
give, 29
gnosco (nosco) , 11, 58
gnostic, 58
God, 11, 15, 56, 68, 101, 105f.

god-spell, 93
Golden Mean, the, 6
good, 3, 32, 70, 78
good angel, 73
good will, 102
gospel, 93
governor, 87f.
grace, 102f.
grade, 68
graduate, 68
gradus, 68
Grand Lodge, 8
gratia, 102
gravity, 42
Great Mother, 44
guberno, 87

habit, 24, 71
habitus, 71
hand, 41
hap, 66
happen, 32
happenstance, 66, 95
happiness, 67, 77
have, 40
health, 41, 71
heath-dweller, 86
heathen, 86
heliotropic, 47
heretic, 99
hero, 76, 107
heterodox, 74
history, 9f., 87
Holy Spirit, 46
Homoiousian, 33
homonym, 48
Homoousian, 33
hope, 104
human being, 56
human nature, 25
humility, 92
humor, 71
humus, 92
hylo-, 33
hylomorphism, 38, 44
hylozoist, 44
hypocrite, 94
hypostasis, 98f.
hypothesize, 38

icon, 17
idea, 17, 19, 22
ideal, 17, 73
idealis, 17
idealism, 19, 51
idiom, 57

"IDIOS (ἴδιος) , 72
idiot, 72
idol, 17
illumination, 14
image, 18f., 21
imagination, 19, 96
imago, 18
imitators, 91
imitor, 81
immanent, 108
immoral, 71
impel, 64
imperare (impero) , 84
implico, 6
impressions, 16, 28
inclosure, 86
indemnification, 99
indivisible, 31
indoctrinate, 73
inductio, 60
inductive, 60
infallibility, 99
infer, 60
inference, 60
infero, 60
inform, 15
ingenium, 56
ingenious, 56
ingenuity, 79
injustice, 76
in-maneo (immaneo) , 108
innate, 56
innovation, 74, 91
insight, 60, 62, 69
insinuate, 48
inspiration, 40, 96
in-statuo, 75
instigo, 65
instinct, 65
institution, 75, 94
instrument, 56
instrumentalist, 69
intellectual, an, 72
intelligence, 61f.
intelligens, 61
intelligo, 61f.
inter-lego, 62
in-tueor, 61
intuition, 60f., 69, 109
involve, 6
"ISTEMI (ἴστημι) , 57
'ISTORÍA (ἱστορία) , 10

jacio, 31
Jehovah, 12, 105f.
join, 41

Joss, 107
joss-sticks, 107
jour, 107
journal, 107
Jove, 106
Judgment, 100f.
Jupiter, 106
jus, juris, 75
justice, 75, 102
Kaiser, 84
KATÁ (κατά) , 24
KEÎMAI (κεῖμαι) , 31
kin, 25f.
kind, 23, 25
kindness, 102
KINÉO (κινέω) , 8
kinesthesia, 8
king, 84
kinship, 57, 61
kith, 26
know, 57f.
KRATÉO (κρατέω) , 84
KRÍSIS (κρίσις) , 75
KUBERNÁO (κυβερνάω) , 88
Kunst, 58

label, 22, 24, 26, 28
labor, 40
language, 9f.
lasciviousness, 103
lascivus, 103
last, 89
law, 74f.
legalis, 76
legislator, 75
lego, 61
LÉGO (λέγω) , 11, 24, 59, 61
letter, 86
lex, legis, 75
libeo, 77
liberal, 58, 77, 81
libertine, 77
liberty, 77
libidinous, 103
libido, 77
libra, 65
libro, 65
lie, 31
lieben, 103
life, 44
light, 14
like, 33, 56
limit, 39
lingo, 10
lingua, 10
logic, 59f.

116

LOGIKÓS (λογικός), 59
logomachy, 11
LÓGOS (λόγος), 10f., 35, 52, 59, 61
loial, 76
love, 44, 78, 102f.
loyal, 76
luceo, 14
lucidity, 17
luck, 66
lumen, 14
lust, 103

MÁCHE (μάχη), 11
machine, 55f.
madman, 72
magister, 88
magister populi, 88
magnanimous, 88
magnate, 88
magnus, 88
Mahatma, 97
MAÍNOMAI (μαίνομαι), 96
make, 41, 71
Mandarin, 69
mania, 96
manliness, 76
MANTHÁNO (μανθάνω), 54
MÁNTIS (μάντις), 96
manu (manus), 41
manu-facere, 41
manufacture, 41
many, 82
mark, 20
mass, 34, 82, 86
master, 88
mater, 44
materia, 44
materialism, 34, 44, 51, 56
materialize, 22
mathematics, 54f.
MATHETÉS (μαθητής), 54
matrix, 44
matter, 29f., 33, 37f., 44, 64, 99
maturity, 41
mean, 13
measure, 75
MECHANÁOMAI (μηχανάομαι), 55
MECHANÉ (μηχανή), 55
MÊCHOS (μῆχος), 55
mediate, 60
mediator, 69
meditation, 69, 109
meditor, 69
medius, 60
MÉDOMAI (μέδομαι), 61
MEIDÁO (μειδάω), 97

memory, 13
mental force, 68
meo, 71
Messiah, 98
metamorphosis, 65
METANOÉO (μετανοέω), 99
METAPHÉRO (μεταφέρω), 48
metaphor, 48f., 52f., 57f., 64f.
metonym, 51
metonymy, 48, 54
METRÉO (μετρέω), 27
middle, 60
middle class, 77
midwife, 73
MIMÉOMAI (μιμέομαι), 18, 81
mimic, 18, 81
mind, 13, 16, 55, 58
miracle, 97
miraculum, 97
mirage, 97
miror, 97
mister, 88
MNÉME (μνήμη), 13
mob, 83f.
mobile (mobilis), 83
mode, 75
modest, 75
modestus, 75
modus, 75
monism, 51
MÓNOS (μόνος), 84
monsieur, 88
monsignor, 88
moral, 71
mores (pl. of mos), 71
morose, 71
morosus, 71
MORPHÉ (μορφή), 15, 38
MORPHÓ (μορφόω), 15
morphology, 15, 24
mos, moralis, 71ff.
mother, 44
motion, 63
movement, 92
multitude, the, 82
munificent, 79
munificius, 79
munus, 79
muscle, 4f., 42
musculus, 4
MYO (μύο), 44, 98
MYSTÉRION (μυστήριον), 98
mystery, 44, 96, 98f.
myth, 10, 97
MYTHOS (μῦθος), 10, 97

117

name, 11, 24, 28, 48f.
nascor, 25
natura, 52
natural philosophy, 25
nature, 24, 37, 39, 81
NÉMO (νέμω), 27
neophyte, 8
NÉOS (νέος), 8
nephew, 87
nepos, 87
nepotism, 87
nomen, 11
NOMÍA (νομία), 24
NÓMOS (νόμος), 24
nosco, 11, 17, 58
notio, 17
notion, 17, 57
notionate, 17

office, 79
OIDA (οἶδα), 58
'OIKONOMÍA (οἰκονομία), 27
OIKOS (οἶκος), 27
old man, 87
oligarchy, 84
'OLÍGOI, OI (ὀλίγοι, οἱ), 84
'OLÍGOS (ὀλίγος), 84
omens, 95
omnipotence, 101
omniscience, 101
"OMOIOS (ὅμοιος), 33
'OMÓS (ὁμός), 33
one, 69, 84, 101
"ONOMA (ὄνομα), 48f.
onomatopoeia, 49
"ONTA, TÁ (ὄντα, τά), 35
ontology, 3, 35
opera, 40
operation, 40
opposite, 86
oracles, 95
orator, 86
order, 84
organ, 7, 55f.
"ORGANON (ὄργανον), 7, 55
origin, 26
ornament, 78
oro, 95
orthodox, 74
'ORTHÓS (ὀρθός), 74
'OUSÍA (οὐσία), 32f., 39
outbirth, 109
outlaws, 72
outsider, 72
over, 57
" over-stand," 57

padre, 87
pagan, 86, 103
pagus, 86
PAIDAGOGÓS (παιδαγωγός), 73
pain, 43
PAÎS (παῖς), 73
PALÁME (παλάμη), 8
palm, 8
papa, 87
PARÁ (παρά), 49
parable, 49f., 52f., 97
PARABOLÉ (παραβολή), 49
parabolic, 97
parallel, 49
partner, 41
PÁSCHO (πάσχω), 67
passion, 67
passive, 67
pater, 87
paternal, 86
paternalism, 87
PATHEÎN (παθεῖν), 67
pathetic, 67
patience, 67
patient, 67
patior, 67
patrician, 87
patriot, 87
pattern, 21
pays, 86
peasant, 86
pebble, 53
pedagogue, 73
pello, 64
pellucid, 14
penalty, 99
penchant, 48
people, the, 82
PERÁO (περάω), 7
perception, 57
percipio (for *per-capio*), 57
per-facio, 68
perfect, 68f.
perfection, 41, 108
perficio (for *per-facio*), 41, 108
perform, 24, 39
person, 93
persona, 93
perspiration, 40
PHAÍNO (φαίνω), 14
phantasm, 14
PHANTÁZO (φαντάζω), 14
phenomena, 14, 28
PHÉRO (φέρω), 48, 63
philander, 103
philanthropy, 103

118

PHILÉO (φιλέω), 103f.
philology, 103
PHÍLOS (φίλος), 103
philosophy, 103
PHÓBOS (φόβος), 85
PHÔS (φῶς), 47
phototropic, 47
PHYLON (φῦλον), 25
phylum, 25f.
PHYO (φύω), 25, 37
PHYSIS (φύσις), 25f., 37, 81
PHYTOS (φύτος), 8
pictura, 19
picture, 19
pingo, 19
place, 30
placing, 30
playwright, 86
plebeian, 82, 87
plebs, 82
plethora, 82
PLÊTHOS (πλῆθος), 82
PLOÚTOI, OI (πλοῦτοι, οἱ), 84
plow, 85
plumage, 78
plutocracy, 84
PNÉO (πνέω), 40
PNEÛMA (πνεῦμα), 40
pneumatic, 40
pneumonia, 40
PODÓS (πούς, ποδός), 26
poena, 99
poet, 48, 54f., 86, 96
poetry, 47, 48, 55
POIÉO (ποιέω), 49
PÓLIS (πόλις), 86f.
politics, 86f.
POLLOÍ, OI (πολλοί, οἱ), 82
POLÚS (πολύς), 82
pono, 30
pontifex maximus, 87
pope, 87
populace, 82
populus, 82, 84
potens, 7, 68
potent, 7, 68
potential, 68
potentiality, 7, 56, 67, 99
power, 64, 68
practice, 7
prae-dico, 32, 93
praett, 79
PRÂGMA (πρᾶγμα), 7
pragmatist, 69
PRÁSSO (ποάσσω), 7
preach, 32

preacher, 93
predestination, 101
predicate, 32
pre-established, 96
prehensile, 57
PRÉSBYS (πρέσβυς), 93
presbyterian, 87, 93
PRESBYTEROS (πρεσβύτερος), 93
PRESBYTES (πρεσβύτης), 87
press, the, 83
pretty, 79
price, 77
priest, 92f., 101
primus, 90
prince, 90
princeps, 90
principal, 90
principle, 90, 95
print, 21
proclaim, 32
produce, 25, 37, 81
progressive education, 73
propel, 64
property, 32
PRÓ-PHEMI (πρόφημι), 93
prophet, 48, 72, 92f.
pro-pono, 66
proportio, 54
proportion, 53f.
prosaic, 47
prose, 47f.
prosus, 47
PRÓTE 'OUSÍA (πρώτη ὀυσία), 38
providence, 67
pro-video, 67
prudence, 67
prudens, 67
PSYCHÉ (ψυχή), 40
psychic, 40
PSYCHO (ψύχω), 40
psychology, 40
psycho-somatic, 43
pun, 2, 52, 54
punishment, 99
punster, 51
puritan, 71
purpose, 39, 66

quality, the, 82

rabble, 83
race, 25
racist, 28
radical, 73, 90
radix, 73
ratio, 53f., 56

ratio, 53f., 56f.
ratiocinatio, 59
ratiocination, 56, 59f.
real, 35f.
reality, 42f.
reason, 56, 59, 60f.
reckon, 53
recognize, 58
recollection, 16, 19
rectitude, 74
rectus, 74
regula, 75
reify, 46, 70
relate, 53
relax, 5
relaxo, 5
ῬΈΟ (ῥέω) , 35f.
reor, 59
repel, 64
repentance, 99
republic, 36
Republicans, 84
res, 35f., 46, 69, 84
respiration, 41
response, 65
responsible, 65
res publica, 36
ῬΈΤΟR (ῥήτωρ) , 86
rhetorician, 86
rich, the, 84
right, 74
righteous, 74f.
ritualist, 94
root, 73
rule, 75, 84
rural, 86
rus, ruris, 86
rustics, 86

sacrament, 98
sacred, 71
same, 33
sancio, 74
sanction, 74
scales, 65
SCHÉMA (σχῆμα) , 16, 69
schematize, 16
scheme, 16, 69
schismatic, 99
SCHÍZO (σχίζω) , 99
schizophrenia, 51, 99
sciences, 24
scientist, 26, 60, 91f., 100
scop, 15
seal, 20
seal-ring, 20

see, 58
seer, 48
select, 79
selego (seligo) , 79
self-righteous, 75
SÉMA (σῆμα) , 13, 20
SEMAÍNO (σημαίνω) , 13
semantic, 13, 20
SEMANTIKÓS (σημαντικός) , 13
semaphore, 13, 20, 97
senator, 87f.
senex, 87
senile, 87
senior, 88
senior, 88
sensation, 8, 57, 78
sense, 4, 8, 29
sensus, 8
sensus communis, 29
shape, 15, 93
share, 41
sigillum, 20
sign, 20f., 28, 64, 97
signal, 20
signature, 19f., 95
signet-ring, 20
significant, 13
signum, 20
silence, 96, 98
simile, 48, 51f.
sin, 100
sinister, 75
sinuosity, 48
sinus, 48
sir, 88
skeptic, 19, 102
slaves, 55
smile, 97
socialists, 85
societas, 85
society, 41, 85
socio, 41
socius, 41, 85
SÔMA (σῶμα) , 43
somatic, 43
SOPHÍA (σοφία) , 103
sorting, 24
soul, 40
space, 28
SPÁO (σπάω) , 5
spasm, 5
spastic, 5
species, 15, 18, 22f., 25
specimens, 26
specio, 14, 61
spectacles, 15

specters, 14
specula, 14
speculate, 15
speculation, 61
speculators, 15
SPÉNDO (σπένδω) , 65
spirit, 40, 46, 64
spiritualization, 22
spiritus, 40, 46
spiro, 40, 46
spoken, 35
spondeo, 65
spontaneous, 55, 65
sponte, 55f., 65
stability, 75
stance, 98
stand, 32, 36, 57, 74
standards, 75
state, 75, 94
statement, 94
statue, 94
statuo, 74
status, 75
status, 75
statutes, 74
sto, 36, 94, 98
stock, 25
story, 10
STRÁGGO (στράγγω) , 5
straight, 74
strain, 5, 64
strange, 85
stretch, 6
stringo, 5, 64
structure, 26
sub, 30
subject, 31, 39
subjectum, 31f.
sublime, 80
sublimis, 80
substance, 28, 32f., 39, 94, 98f.
substantia, 32f.
substantive, 32
substitution, 94
substo, 32
suburb, 85
suffer, 67
sum, 37
superstitio, 94f.
superstition, 94f.
superus, 107
suppose, 30
supreme, 107
syllogism, 59f.
SYLLOGÍSOMAI (συλλογίζομαι) , 59
SYMBÁLLO (συμβάλλω) , 21

symbol, 20f., 28, 50, 53, 58
symbolizing, 64
SYMBOLON (σύμβολον) , 21
synecdoche, 49, 51
synonym, 48
systematize, 16

taceo, 46
taciturnity, 46
taecean, 95
TÀ MATHÉMATA (τὰ μαθήματα) , 54f
tangent, 51
tango, 51
TÁSSO (τάσσω) , 24
tautology, 14
TÁXIS (τάξις) , 24
taxonomist, 26
taxonomy, 24
teach, 95
teacher, 73
TÉCHNE (τέχνη) , 81
TEÍNO (τείνω) , 5
TÉKNON (τέκνον) , 81
TEKÓN (τεκών) , 81
TÉLOS (τέλος) , 40, 91
TÉMNO (τέμνω) , 69
temple, 69
templum, 69
tendo, 5
tense, 5
tensility, 5
tension, 5
terminal, 66
terminus, 66
tetanus, 5
Tetragrammaton, 105f.
THAÛMA (θαῦμα) , 97
THAUMÁDZO (θαυμάζω) , 97
THEÁOMAI (θεάομαι) , 8, 61
theatre, 61
theist, 106
theodicy, 106
theologians, 101f., 109
theology, 106, 109
theorize, 61
theory, 8
THEÓS (θεός) , 106
THÉSIS (θέσις) , 30
thing, 36, 84
Thor, 107
ticket, 22
TÍKTO (τίκτω) , 81
token, 20, 95
tone, 5
tongue, 10

121

tonic, 5
tonicity, 5
τὸ PLÊTHOS (τὸ πλῆθος), 82
touch, 8, 50
touchée, 50
touchstone, 50
township, 86
trace, 21
traditions, 75
trado, 75
transcendent, 108
transcendo, 108
translation, 18, 48
transmit, 75
transubstantiation, 34, 94, 98f.
Trinity, the, 33, 37, 98
trope, 47f.
TRÓPOS (τρόπος), 47
truth, 3
twists of the tongue, 46f.
type, 21
TYPOS (τύπος), 21

"ULE (ὕλη), 33, 38, 44
unconventional, 72
uncouth, 58
uncut, 31
under, 30f.
understand, 57, 94
universe, 28, 69, 95
univocal, 12, 54, 109
unknown, 95
unus, 85
'UPÓ (ὑπό), 30
'UPOKEÍMENON, TÒ (ὑποκείμενον, τὸ)
    31
'UPÓSTASIS (ὑπόστασις), 32, 39
upright, 74f.
urbanity, 85
urbs, 85
urvo, 85

vale, 76
valere (valeo), 76
valiant, 76
valor, 64
value, 76f.
vengeance, 101

verbum, 10
vernacular, 83
vernaculus, 83
via negativa, 109
video, 61
vigorous, 76
vir, 64, 76, 102
virtue, 64, 67, 76, 96
virtus, 76
vision, 14, 61
voco, 9
voice, 9
voice of the people, 82
volens, 66
volentia, 66
volo, 66
voluntary, 66
vox, 9
vulgar, 83
vulgate, 83
vulgus, 83
vulgus mobile, 83

wealth, 32, 77
weorth, 77
what, 92
why, 92
wilderness, 96
will, 66, 68, 71
wisdom, 61
wise, 14
wish, 66
womb, 44
wood, 33
word, 10, 35, 90
work, 40, 55
world, 12
worth, 77
wrath, 101

xenophobia, 85
XÉNOS (ξένος), 85

Yawe, 106

ZEÚS (Ζεύς), 106
ZOÉ (ζωή), 44